How come THAT idiot's rich and I'm not?

Robert Shemin

Crown Publishers   New York

Copyright © 2008 by Robert Shemin

Published in the United States by Crown Publishers, an imprint of the Crown
Publishing Group, a division of Random House, Inc., New York.
www.crownpublishing.com

Crown is a trademark and the Crown colophon is a registered trademark of
Random House, Inc.

Library of Congress Cataloging-in-Publication Data

Shemin, Robert, 1963–
    How come THAT idiot's rich and I'm not? / Robert Shemin.—1st ed.
        p. cm.
    1. Finance, Personal—Psychological aspects.   2. Wealth—Psychological
aspects.   3. Goal (Psychology)   4. Adaptability (Personality trait)   5. Success
in business—Psychological aspects.   I. Title.
    HG179.S4614 2007
    332.024—dc22   2007032526

ISBN: 978-0-307-39507-8

Printed in the United States of America

Design by Leonard Henderson

10 9 8 7 6 5 4 3 2 1

First Edition

Dedicated
to my son, Alexander

Acknowledgments

No one ever succeeds alone, and the creation of this book is no exception. I'd like to take this space to acknowledge and thank all those people who came together as an amazing team to bring it to life.

Edita Kaye, my friend and business partner in this venture, without whose vision, drive, and sheer hard work this book wouldn't have happened. She was instrumental in clarifying the original concept, refining the proposal, seeking out the very best literary agent in the world, and serving as my writing partner. She's as dedicated and committed as I am to helping millions live their perfect lives—rich in all the gifts of the Universe.

Larry Kirshbaum, my literary agent. You believed in my message and shared your amazing editorial talents and insights every step of the way. Your professionalism, encouragement, and enthusiasm made this project a joy. You brought out the very best in this book. I am proud to call you my agent and my friend.

Rick Horgan, my brilliant and insightful editor at Crown Publishers. Thank you for your belief in and enthusiasm for this book. Your outstanding editorial comments and suggestions, coupled with your sharp pencil, brought focus and clarity to the manuscript. You've been such a positive influence in this process and I thank you for your dedication in bringing this message of wealth to the world.

Barbara McNichol, my copy editor and editorial angel. Thank you, Barbara, for your assembly of data and your patient attention to detail as well as checking and double-checking facts. Your keen editing eye and professional skill have greatly contributed to the book's final polish.

I wish to also thank the talented team at Crown Publishers whose enthusiasm for the project and creativity in bringing it to the reading public are unsurpassed. Special thanks must go to Tina Constable, vice president and publisher, Crown; Kristin Kiser, editorial director; Philip Patrick, publisher, Three Rivers Press, and director of marketing,

Crown; Donna Passannante, marketing director; Christine Aronson, director of publicity; Tara Delaney Gilbride and Sarah Breivogel, publicity managers; Linda Kaplan, director, subsidiary rights; Shawn Nicholls, online marketing manager; and all the other wonder folks at Crown who worked so hard for this book.

Verena Wagner, my dedicated assistant, merits thanks as well. She keeps my life organized and my schedule uncluttered, and makes sure that whether I'm on the road speaking or at home coaching, my professional life runs smoothly.

Bill Zanker, founder and chairman, The Learning Annex, thanks for all the great opportunities to help so many people across the country; and Samantha Del Canto, executive vice president, thanks for your unflagging enthusiasm and support.

Brian McAdams, chairman, EMS, and all the special people who have helped and supported me; Derek, Bruce, Cindi, Chad, and Lona were there for me every day.

Thanks to David Early, CEO, Dynetech, for all the seminars and promotion, as well as Larry Pino, chairman and founder, and all the other special people at Dynetech.

A very special thanks to my great friends and fellow Rich Idiots Dan Davidson, Anthony Cherry, and Patrick and Kerry James.

Dr. Albert Lowry deserves a big thank-you for being a great friend and teacher.

I would also like to thank my family; my parents, Lillian and Jules Shemin, as well as Randy, Kim, and Rochelle—thanks for being there.

Reb Chaim—thank you. You have helped me in ways that cannot be counted.

My other great friends, mentors, and teachers including, but not limited to, Lisa Delman, who introduced me to people who have changed my life; Master Tseng for his great teachings; Dr. Richard Hirsch for keeping me laughing and healthy.

Thanks also to Paul Bauer and all the real-estate investor associations, and most especially to the million-plus people and students who took their time to hear me speak.

And if you're reading this, I want to thank you for the opportunity, because without you none of this would be happening.

Contents

Part THREE

FIRE

Read Me First!

There is always room at the top.
— DANIEL WEBSTER

Got that? There's *always* room at the top.

Congratulations. You've just taken your first step on that staircase to the place you've always wanted to be. You know the upward journey I'm talking about. It's the one where you start off all alone in the dark on the bottom step in a pair of ratty jeans and a T-shirt. By the time you reach that top step you're all decked out in designer threads, with an attractive companion on your arm, a full orchestra playing, champagne bubbles popping everywhere, hundred-dollar bills floating down from the ceiling, and grand-finale fireworks.

But this isn't a movie. This is real. And in buying this book you've just done one of the smartest real things you'll ever do.

It probably doesn't feel that way, though. Rather, you're probably afraid this will end up being just another "how to get rich as fast as possible with as little effort as possible" book, like the other dozen you've already bought, read, and tossed. I understand your skepticism. And yet I know that there'll come a point as you're turning these pages when the light begins to dawn.

I'd love to see your face when you "get it"—the one simple thing you were doing all wrong that has blocked real wealth for you. I'd love to be a fly on the wall when you exhale and say, "Wow." That's the moment when you'll discover you've got "rich" inside you already, that you've had it all along, and that all you have to do is let it out.

1

I wish I could be invisible at your dinner table, or in the break room in your office, when you start sharing with your friends and co-workers the seven secrets you really knew all the time—but somehow "forgot" under the weight of just living every day and making ends meet. I wish I could be there when you start climbing that staircase to meet your future wealth.

Let me give you a sneak peek at what you're going to experience as you plunge further into this book. Ready? I've divided this book into three really simple parts.

1. Part One is "Ready." This is the part that gets you into the Rich Idiot space fast.
2. Part Two is "Aim." The material in this section is like a MapQuest diagram to wealth. Once you program in your wealth path, you'll have a straight shot to riches.
3. Part Three is "Fire." Here's where you pull the trigger, take your shot, and hit the target!

Let me explain each of these in a little more detail.

Part One

Right away in Chapter 1 you're going to learn the one thing about yourself that's been keeping you broke. And you're going to learn how to unblock it. No waiting.

But there's more. You're going to discover how easy it is to become a Rich Idiot. You're going to kick yourself when you realize you've had (as we all have) the Rich Idiot seed inside all along and could have been a Rich Idiot years ago. But hey, as the famous writer George Eliot said, "It's never too late to be what you might have become." So I'll show you exactly what happened to that seed of wealth potential—why it never grew and broke through the soil to stretch toward the sunshine of wealth. I'll also show you how to quickly and easily enrich that seed, unlocking its potential.

Don't worry about having to learn a lot of stuff. You'll quickly see that this Rich Idiot book isn't about learning; it's about *unlearning*. You're going to unlearn all the things that have trapped you in a paycheck-to-paycheck life.

Wait until you take the Rich Idiot Test. This is the one about the giraffe in the refrigerator. Your answers will determine how quickly you can transition from an eight-year-old car, two mortgages, and three jobs to a brand-new sports car, a fabulous house, and no job at all!

By the time you've finished the first chapter you'll know how to complete this key sentence: "Rich Idiots don't work for money, they work for _____!"

You'll also learn how I became a Rich Idiot. Here I'll confide secrets I've never shared with anyone before—not the hundreds of thousands who crowd into my seminars, not the hundreds of thousands who've read my previous books. These are the stories I have kept just for you.

If the first chapter opens your mind to the wealth that's just waiting up ahead, the second chapter opens your heart and soul.

There isn't a single Rich Idiot out there who hasn't followed the spiritual laws of wealth. And when I use the term "spiritual laws" don't think I'm referring to "woo-woo" stuff you can just skip over. There's real power here. Break these spiritual laws of wealth and stay broke. Believe them, have faith in them, follow them, and your rewards will be without limit.

Part Two

This part is all about you and your personal path to riches.

I guarantee a huge shock when you read about Rich Idiots and their goals. You won't believe it. All those goals you've been writing down for years—I'm going to tell you why you're not reaching them.

From there I'm going to show you how to live your rich life right now. I mean *right now*, as in today. Not only am I going to show you exactly what to do to immediately live like a Rich Idiot, I'm going to prove to you that if you *don't* begin to live rich today, chances are you won't get rich tomorrow. Next I'm going to let you in on the secret of O.P. Power (Other People Power). I'm going to help you find the people who will be your wealth "angels."

By the time you've finished this part of the book, you're going to look like a Rich Idiot, live like one, dress like one, travel like one, and have your very own set of Rich Idiot friends and helpers. You'll have entered the golden circle. You'll be ready for Part Three, where you'll attain full Rich Idiot status.

Part Three

In this part you're going to pull the trigger. You're going to become a member of the Rich Idiot Club, with all the perks. In Part Three you're going to start up that fantastic staircase—two, even three steps at a time—and I'm going to be there, waiting to greet you at the top!

I can hear *yeah, buts* already, and I want you to silence them here and now. There *are* no *yeah, buts*. I know you're reading this book and maybe there's this huge pile of bills you're dealing with. I know you may have too much debt. I know you're probably tired of money pressures and perhaps even a little scared. How do I know that? Because I've been there and—surprise, surprise—so has every other Rich Idiot I know. So relax. If you're broke, worried sick, in debt, or just frustrated about where you stand moneywise, that's no problem. It just means you're on your way to becoming one of us!

The first thing I'm going to do in Part Three is get you out of debt. And I don't want to hear any objections. You got into debt—okay, that's the bad news. The *good* news is that you can get out. I've helped thousands and thousands of people who were just as overwhelmed, exhausted, and frightened as you.

Once we get that debt stuff taken care of, I'm going to talk about some very important things called assets. We all know what assets are, but which are the best three and how do you get them—fast? I'll cover all that, and then I'm going to let you in on the four deadly D's—the enemies of Rich Idiot assets and how to zap them before they zap you.

But I'm not going to stop there. Next, I'm going to walk you through the act chapter. This is the "take action" bit. This is where you're standing with your toes curled around the edge of a diving board. You're absolutely terrified. The pool of wealth seems so far below. It seems like you might miss it entirely. You don't want to jump. So I'm going to come up behind you and give you that push.

What's going to happen? You're going to execute a perfect dive, and when you break through the surface, guess what? You'll be a Rich Idiot! A little wet, but a Rich Idiot nevertheless. And believe me, you'll want to get right back up there on that diving platform and jump in again—this time all by yourself.

But your Rich Idiot secrets don't end here. In my dealing I always like to give more, and this book is no exception—which means I'll be adding a bonus chapter: Secret No. 8!

Thought that was it, did you? Well, not quite. Here's one more thing you'll be able to take with you on your Rich Idiot journey.

Web Site Resources

To get where you want to go you'll frequently have need of resources, organizations, Web links, and phone numbers. So I've provided as many as possible. Use them. My Web site can be located at:

www.GetRichWithRobert.com

According to U.S. Census data, there are more than four million households in America with a net worth above $1 million.

Why couldn't one of them be yours?

part **ONE**

READY

secret no. 1

Turn Everything You Ever Thought About Getting Rich Upside Down

He dares to be a fool and that is the first step in the direction of wisdom.
— JAMES GIBBONS HUNEKER

The Rich Idiot Test

I'm going to give you a sneak peek at my famous Rich Idiot Test. Go ahead. Start.

1. How do you put a giraffe into a refrigerator?
2. How do you put an elephant into the refrigerator?
3. The Lion King is hosting an animal conference. All of the animals attend the animal conference, except one. Which animal is not there?
4. You have to cross a river. The river is used by dangerous crocodiles. You do not have a boat. How do you manage it?

Want to know how well you did? How close you are to becoming a Rich Idiot? Read on.

The Scenarios

It's happened to all of us. You're stuck in the one lane that's not moving when some guy whizzes past in a brand-new Cadillac or Porsche.
He flashes a Rolex. Suddenly you recognize him: He's the idiot who
flunked out of your school. You studied hard and got straight A's, and
now you're sitting in an eight-year-old car wearing a knockoff watch.
In that moment you ask, "If I'm so smart, how come that idiot's rich
and I'm not?"

Or how about this: You pick up a copy of the local paper and see a
photo of a guy shaking hands with the governor. Seems he turned his
"nothing" business into a holding company. Now he has interests in
every major city in the state and about five thousand people working
for him. That's when you realize he used to be that kid who always got
the change wrong when he came to collect the newspaper money. You
never got the money wrong. Yet now the only person who ever shakes
your hand is the greeter at Wal-Mart. You ask, "If I'm so dependable,
how come that idiot's rich and I'm not?"

Or this: You've finally purchased your first home. You and your
wife can just about make the payments if you both work full-time and
give up all thoughts of a family. One day your friends drag you to a
business-opportunity meeting with three hundred other wannabe-rich
hopefuls. That's when you realize the guy standing on the stage tossing hundred-dollar bills into the crowd is the son of your mom's
neighbor in Queens who was always borrowing money off everyone to
buy candy because he never had a dime. You've never ever borrowed
anything—not even a penny—not once. You always paid your own way.
And now you're living paycheck to paycheck and all *you've* got in your
pocket is $87.62 and your lucky coin. You can't help but ask, "If I was
always so careful about money, how come that idiot's rich and I'm not?"

How about this one: You're standing in the checkout line at the su-
permarket and skimming the covers of the magazines, thinking you'd
like to buy a couple, only cash is tight right now. There on the cover of
People—you suddenly see it—a small inset photo that looks really

familiar. You grab the magazine and flip to the page. Sure enough, there's a long story about this woman who just donated a zillion dollars to an organization that helps women build businesses. You read on. Turns out she became a fashion designer, launched a hugely successful Internet clothing empire, and adopted three orphans from poverty-stricken countries. More than that, she accomplished all this by the age of thirty! You just passed the forty-one-year mark. Worst of all, you realize that the woman with the great *People* magazine life was that weird kid you used to babysit for a few dollars. She was the one who wore purple tights with ragged holes in the knees topped off with a mustard yellow T-shirt and a blue, pink, and orange striped pajama top. You always matched perfectly. Every outfit you wore was impeccably coordinated. You can't help but ask, "If I was always so correct, how come that idiot's got this terrific creative life, and I'm standing at the checkout counter worrying about the price of a couple of magazines?"

Here's one more: You've just been promoted to V.P. of something worthwhile. It only cost you ten years of eighty-hour weeks and one marriage, but you made it. You're rewarded with a trip to the annual industry conference. Then your world turns upside down. You recognize the keynote speaker—he's the guy who flunked out halfway through your senior year. Worse, you recognize the woman sitting beside him. She dropped out because she got pregnant. The only ones you don't recognize are the three handsome children sitting beside them on the stage. Now the whole family is getting a standing ovation because they just endowed a chair, built a hospital, funded two labs, and bought milk for an entire country. And the two parents who everyone said wouldn't last six months have got this great family and this great life. You, on the other hand, went to an Ivy League school on a full scholarship and spent the last ten years taking course after course so you could climb up the corporate ladder. Your wife divorced you four years ago and you see your kids every other weekend for a few hours. You ask, "If I work so hard and I'm so smart, how come the universe is doling out these lavish gifts to people who broke all the rules? How come those idiots have it all and my family and I don't?"

What Are You Doing Wrong?

You know the question: *How come THAT idiot's rich and I'm not?* Or put another way: How come *that* idiot's living your dream life and you're not—despite all your smarts and hard work? How come that idiot's able to build a business while you're slogging your life away in some anonymous cubicle, working for a corporation you're beginning to feel doesn't really care about you? How come that idiot's been able to turn his or her talents and dreams into a life of wealth while your talents and dreams are packed away in the back of your closet, along with those golf clubs you never have time to use and that scuba gear that's getting brittle because you never even take a weekend off, much less indulge yourself and your family in a tropical-island vacation? How come that idiot's able to send his kids to the best schools while you're worried about paying for a state school? How come that idiot's able to give his family financial security while you're always just making ends meet? And how come that idiot's able to make a real difference in people's lives—change the world even—while you're plodding along, just another increasingly unsatisfied, hardworking, and dependable wealth-seeking wannabe?

The answer is so simple it's scary.

What made that guy or that girl back then an idiot are the same qualities that are making them rich today. And what got you the good grades and the pats on the back and all the gold stars is what's keeping you from getting rich.

Duh! And you thought it was all about hard work, sticking to the rules, and never coloring outside the lines—hello?

So what can you do about it?

This book can change all that. It can make real wealth happen for you—the kind that enables you to do whatever you want without worrying about money, take care of your loved ones, and have plenty left over to make the world a better place for others. But first you have to ask yourself a really tough question: Deep down inside, do I really want to be rich?

To be more specific, are you willing to do—or, rather, *undo*—all the things that have kept you from acquiring your first fortune? Are you willing not to learn, but to *unlearn*, the thinking and working habits of a lifetime?

If you're ready to turn your world upside down, then you're ready to get rich with Robert.

Why follow my lead?

Because I myself started as one of those "idiots" who, by a process of trial and error, was lucky enough to discover the seven secrets I'm about to share with you, and to follow them to wealth.

My Rich Idiot Beginnings

I grew up in Nashville, Tennessee, and attended Hillwood High. I didn't get straight A's, become valedictorian, or rake in scholarships to top colleges. The reality is, I graduated practically at the very bottom of my class—probably 424 out of 425. My attendance record was so poor (I skipped about thirty-seven straight days in my senior year) that the Board of Education called to revoke my diploma, but it was too late. My own parents had already taken it away from me, saying I didn't deserve it.

As it turns out, my schooling wasn't a total loss. I was unaware at the time that while I was flunking those middle and high school tests I was actually honing what would become my set of "Rich Idiot skills."

You see, at age fifteen I took a job as a busboy in a local restaurant. The other busboys were happy to be called busboy. Not me. The first thing I did was change my job title to Table Maintenance Engineer. Hey, don't knock it. It got laughs—and also more respect and bigger tips.

Soon I had moved up the ladder to waiter or, as I called myself, Table Service Specialist. Now I was bringing in over $800 a week—more than my teachers were averaging at the time.

What I didn't know then was that the characteristics I displayed would bring me immense success later in life. For example:

I wanted control over my income.

I showed pride in my work, and gave myself titles that reflected that pride.

I valued real cash money that I could see and touch over the invisible money that showed up on a pay stub.

I learned how to deal well with people—from the temperamental cook to the dissatisfied customer.

These became some of the future building blocks of my own fortune.

How about you? Have you ever gritted your teeth at the title you wore and wished it were more important? Have you ever felt that satisfying wad of cash in your wallet and the surge of confidence it gives? Have you ever succeeded in reaching a goal? Remember how good it was to feel pride and satisfaction in your accomplishments? Rich Idiots feel that way all the time, and you can, too.

My Own Shrink Story

I was such an idiot in school that the administration decided I should see a psychiatrist. The problem was my grades. I never did much of the assigned reading. I didn't do all my homework. I always spoke up in class and didn't follow rules very well. They thought I was an idiot. To validate this view, they sent me to the school shrink.

What they didn't realize was that I was just bored with the assigned books; in fact, I was an avid "secret reader." So in preparation for my first experience with the school psychologist, I borrowed psychology books from my cousin who was in college at the time. My goal was to fool the expert. I *wanted* him to think I was an idiot—crazy as a loon. When he pulled out the Rorschach inkblot test, I was ready for him. I'd read that crazy people identify every inkblot as a bat, so I pointed out a lot of bats. The diagnosis came back as predicted: "Robert is an idiot—he's crazy."

How did that bring me closer to my success? I gained self-confidence from knowing I *could* read, as long as the subject matter excited and moved me. I read books about science, mathematics, astronomy, and history. I explored the world of ideas by devouring books on philosophy and exploration. But my favorite books were biographies. I loved tracing the life path of amazing people.

My Hidden Disabilities Helped Me Become a Rich Idiot

After that, things in school went from bad to worse. I remember the day my typing teacher called me an idiot. I'd failed a typing test for the fiftieth time, and she actually threw a book at me, declaring I would never amount to anything. I simply couldn't type. I didn't know why I made more mistakes than anyone else in the class. I just couldn't get the letters right—couldn't even remember where they were on the keyboard.

Many years later I learned that I have a rare form of dyslexia in which spatial abilities are impaired. That meant I couldn't *use* a keyboard even if I practiced for years. The same disability ensured that I couldn't master math. Today, I can't even find my own investment properties on a map!

But even with this disability I went on to own a real-estate empire of over four hundred properties and to write ten best-selling books. I didn't realize until later the gift this typing teacher had given me. By calling me an idiot she forced me to find other pathways to achieve what I desired. If I couldn't write, I would talk. And talking—public speaking—made me a fortune. When my speeches were transcribed and turned into books, I made another fortune.

Remember!
Rich Idiots never think or say, "I can't." They ask, "How can I?" Take the word *can't* out of your vocabulary.

The Day I Tested the System

Yes, I kept getting idiot grades in school. But deep down I believed I wasn't as big an idiot as all my teachers made me out to be. I'd concluded that the system was at fault. So one day I tested my theory. The class assignment was "Write a poem." I painstakingly copied out a poem from a collection that had won the 1950 Pulitzer Prize and handed it in. Surely, I thought, any poem that had won the coveted Pulitzer would get an A from my English teacher. Wrong. It came back to me with a D. When I challenged the grading system, claiming it was unfair and prejudicial, I got suspended for being—you guessed it—an idiot!

At the time, I didn't realize that I'd just received my first lesson in labels and how hard they are to peel off. My teacher stuck the label of "idiot" on me, and it wouldn't peel off no matter what I did. Other teachers read that label and believed it was accurate. Except deep down I knew otherwise. I held on to self-belief as I made first one, then another, and then a third fortune.

> **Let me apologize and ask forgiveness for any heartache I might have caused my parents or my teachers. Rich Idiots always take responsibility for their actions.**

But I realized this: *The power of self-belief always trumps the power of what others believe about you.*

How about you? Have you ever believed there was much more to you than others seemed to see? Have you ever said to yourself, "One day I'll show them what I can accomplish?" Well, guess what: That day is today.

"Baby" Entrepreneur Finds First Success Secret

At the tender age of sixteen I made my first foray into entrepreneurship. I bought a bunch of T-shirts for 50 cents apiece, rented a space at a Saturday flea market, and started selling them for $2 each. I thought I was really smart, making a profit of almost $1.50 on every shirt.

But after a few Saturdays, I realized that selling is hard work. Not only did it take a long time to make a sale, but people kept messing up my nice neat piles of T-shirts. Worse, I was working up a sweat while my buddies, most from wealthier homes than mine, were spending their Saturdays swimming, hanging out, and having fun.

Something had to change. I had to make money, but—more than money—I had to make time. My teenage brain figured that I needed to make the same amount of money in half the time so my richer buddies wouldn't get all the cute girls. I was missing out on the fun of being a teenager because I was spending my quality time earning the money I needed.

So I got the bright idea of putting a huge sign on the stall that said, "Going Out of Business in One Hour—Everything Must Go." Because I wasn't planning to be there long, I stopped straightening out my stock. You guessed it: I sold more in that one hour than I had in the past two Saturdays, sweating in the sun from eight in the morning until six at night. What was even more surprising, I sold more when my T-shirts looked like they were all being pulled apart instead of stacked in folded piles.

I pocketed my cash, closed down my booth, and went swimming and partying with my friends. I repeated the same formula every Saturday for over two years. And every Saturday it worked like a charm. I had the money *and* I had the time. And as a bonus I learned that working smart is better than working hard or working long hours.

It was only later, when I found myself surrounded by good friends, that I realized what a valuable lesson I'd learned at the flea market. I'd learned that wealth isn't only about money—it's about time. It's about Life, with a capital *L*. I'd learned what money can really buy. It can buy precious time, and it can buy the life you dream of for yourself. In my case, on those warm afternoons it gave me the *time* to develop those friendships I'd keep for a lifetime.

My First "Grown-up" Tough Choice

I knew I was different, but I never really fully reflected on how different until one Thanksgiving. I was working in a huge corporation filled with unhappy and stressed-out executives all chasing dollars and sweating to get rich fast. It was the day I made one of the best "mistakes" of my life. I asked my boss for the Friday after Thanksgiving off so I could spend it with my family. At first he didn't say anything. Then he gave me a cold look and asked, "Robert, where are your priorities?" His tone left no doubt that my answer would determine my future at the company. He then said, "Obviously your priorities are not with your career or this company."

That's when it all clicked for me. I saw my future: sitting at my desk in that organization, missing birthdays and anniversaries and all the special moments with my loved ones. Without even thinking, I knew the answer, and the words just spilled out. "You're right. My priorities are not with my career. They're with my family," I replied. At that moment I knew I had to stop working for somebody else.

That was the day I embraced my Rich Idiot self—and I've never looked back. Because on that day I realized that it wasn't only about the money—it was also about the time. It was about how I wanted to spend the life I'd been given and who I wanted to spend that life with. I understood in that instant that money was valueless if it couldn't be used as a lever to create more time.

What about you? How many family events have you missed because of office projects and deadlines imposed on you by someone else? How many bedtime stories haven't you read? How many games of catch haven't you played? How many walks, cuddles, and hugs have you given up while you were busy making money without making time? Not to worry. This book will show you how, by first making more time for yourself and your loved ones, you can make more money than you ever thought possible—the Rich Idiot way.

Remember!
Your priorities should be with your family, friends, relationships, and spiritual pursuits, not with a career. In the end, what else is there?

My Twentieth High School Reunion

My latest idiot story happened just recently, at my twentieth high school reunion. There they all were—the "smart" students with the perfect attendance records and the gold stars—returning twenty years later as burned-out bankers, frustrated corporate executives, and failed entrepreneurs. My three closest buddies were also there—former academic idiots just like me. One has become a top litigator; another owns a chain of businesses across many states; a third was also a self-employed, rich, and happy business owner.

But listen, this gets better.

I ran into my old teacher. (This is one of the teachers that thought I was a complete loser.) He asked, "So, Shemin, what have you done since high school?" I answered, "Well, I've written ten best-selling books; I've spoken to audiences of up to fifty thousand per event all over the country; I've built a personal fortune in real estate; and I've retired twice—the first time at the age of twenty-eight." He smiled at me. And as he walked away I heard him say under his breath, "There's no way. Shemin's still an idiot and still telling stories."

Rich Idiots Are Different

It wasn't until later that I appreciated how important being an idiot was to my success. You see, I was the *different* one. I did everything the wrong way. And that made all the difference. My upside-down way of doing things turned out to be exactly right. It led me to my own wealth and success, and it also brought me something more precious than money—it brought me time. And time is the true measure of wealth. Why do I say that? Because you can always make more money, but you can't make more time.

I hear a lot of stories from the thousands of people I've helped become Rich Idiots through my seminars, and just about every testimonial is about the precious moments wealth has brought with it.

Let me share a couple of the more memorable ones.

Here's Ron's story pretty much as he told it to me: "Robert, just a couple of years ago I was a bartender making $12,000 a year. I was working all the time. I had no family life. My health suffered. I was always in debt. I was always stressed. I knew I had to do something or I'd lose the family I loved. So one day, just like you teach, I joined a network marketing company. I had to. I had no choice. Now, I'm not the smartest guy. I don't have an education. I never finished high school. So when all the instruction books arrived I did exactly what they said to do. I did it day after day—in the few hours I had between my shifts. I didn't think. I kept my mind focused on the instructions and my heart focused on my family. At the end of the first year I'd made $150,000! Now I'm in my fourth year and I'm making about $150,000 a *month*. But the best news is that I have time to spend with my beautiful wife and children. That's what my wealth has brought me—the gift of time." He also said, "A lot of other people who started and were smarter than me quit after just two months. I did not. And things are really good."

I also heard from a woman named Julie. "We were broke," she told me. "Our credit cards were maxed out. We were behind in our mortgage payments. We were both working two jobs each, and still we couldn't make ends meet. Then our daughter won a partial scholarship to a music school. But we couldn't afford the little bit extra that would make her dream of becoming a singer come true. I know you're a parent, so you can imagine how we felt. We were parents and we couldn't give our children what they deserved. That night we ordered your program and never looked back. Our daughter got her music education and our other two children got to go to some really great schools. As for us, our money problems went away and now we have the time to spend together as a family."

The Idiot in Me Made Me Wealthy

Stories like those force this question: Which path do *you* want to take? Do you want to be the hardworking conformist or the Rich Idiot who has plenty of money and the time to enjoy, spend, and share that money with others?

Here's a recap of my choices:

While the other waitstaff were complaining about their jobs giving great service, I was polishing my Table Maintenance Engineer badge, my smile, and my tips.

While everyone else was toeing the line, I was running a series of small businesses that gave me both financial independence and time to cultivate friendships that would last me my whole life.

Because the assigned reading bored me, I happily became a "closet reader" and assigned myself books on subjects that ignited my imagination, desire, and drive.

I had dyslexia and couldn't find my own house on a map, so I was challenged to find other ways to reach my destination.

I appreciated the power of real cash money early.

And I learned that money is only truly satisfying if it's used to buy that most precious of all commodities: time.

Growing up and being called an idiot turned out to be an important factor in my success.

Going from Right Side Up to Upside Down

But enough about me. Let's talk about *you*. If you're reading this book then, I'm guessing, you're not a Rich Idiot—you're what I like to call one of the RUBs: **R**ight side **U**p and **B**roke.

When it comes to wealth, the world *is* upside down. It's not what you *know*, it's what you *don't know* that's the key. The very skills that, early in life, helped you discover what your parents, teachers, and bosses wanted and deliver it is what caused your other skills to atrophy—skills like self-starting and self-direction. The individuals society defines early on as "smart" are good at following orders but lousy at giving themselves orders—and *extremely* lousy at taking charge of their own lives. Meanwhile, those who never fit into the system because they want to drive the bus themselves turn out to have the perfect skill set for building wealth. This explains why that boy who barely squeaked through school or that girl who wore those weird clothes went on to build successful businesses and great fortunes.

What about you? Do you think like a RUB or an idiot? Let's turn your world upside down and find out. Remember the Rich Idiot Test at the very beginning of this chapter? Guess what: Now you get to take it for real.

The Rich Idiot Test

Read each question carefully and write down your answer in the space provided before moving on to the next question.

1. How do you put a giraffe into a refrigerator?

_____

Answer: You open the refrigerator door, put the giraffe in, and close the door. That's how you do it. It's that simple.

If you're like most RUBs, you tend to do very simple things in an overly complicated manner. You'll try to figure out a dozen different ways to accomplish that same simple task—like cutting up the giraffe, folding it over—and all the while you think you're doing everything the right way, the smart way. But you're actually doing it the RUB way—which, as it happens, is the wrong way. You see a fridge. You see a giraffe. You're locked into your "right side up" way of thinking, which says, "Giraffes don't fit into fridges." So you write out complicated formulas involving cubic measurements of refrigeration units. You research surgical techniques for dissecting giraffes. You even investigate consumer and commercial refrigerators. And despite all that learning, you'll still be wrong.

The Rich Idiot isn't burdened by "right side up" ways of thinking. He keeps things simple. The idiot doesn't overthink; he takes the most direct path to the solution—open fridge, shove in giraffe—and he's right.

2. How do you put an elephant into the refrigerator?

Answer: Did you answer, open the refrigerator, put in the elephant, close the door? Good answer, but it's the wrong one. Before you put in the elephant, you have to take out the giraffe. Then put in the elephant and close the door.

This question tests whether you learn from the repercussions of your previous actions. Did you do the same thing—the same wrong RUB thing—even though the situation hasn't materially changed? But it *has* changed, you protest. This time there's a giraffe in the fridge. So? Ask yourself, What *has* changed, really? Nothing has really changed. There is still a fridge and a jungle animal. This should tell you that the same solution as in the first example can be applied to this new example. Problem is, RUBs go right back to the drawing board. Overlearning, but never applying what they already know. What you have been doing up till now is okay but has it gotten you to where you want to be? Are you willing to change a few things to get where you want to go?

Ready to try another?

3. The Lion King is hosting an animal conference. All of the animals attend the animal conference, except one. Which animal does not attend?

Answer: The elephant. You just put the elephant into the fridge, so how can he attend the animal conference?

If you're like most RUBs, all your previous learning is getting in the way of your thinking. You don't link up what you already know. You don't trust your own connections. And where's your sense of playfulness, fun, and that famous "outside the box" thinking?

Here's the last one. Ready?

4. You have to cross a river. The river is used by dangerous crocodiles. You do not have a boat. How do you manage it?

Answer: You swim across the river—all the animals are at the animal conference, remember? And that includes the crocodiles.

Rich Idiots get that right away. They get that there are fewer obstacles to their success, not more. Rich Idiots know that the crocodiles aren't there. So they don't waste any energy worrying about them.

RUBs, on the other hand, don't get wealthy because they worry about things that don't exist—like the crocodiles that aren't even in the river. RUBs overthink, overworry, and overanalyze to the point of inertia. Because they try to imagine every single thing that could go wrong, they never actually move on that moneymaking idea or launch that business venture or sign that offer for their first real-estate investment.

RUBs sit on the banks of an empty river watching for imaginary crocs while all the Rich Idiots swim merrily by.

Welcome to the Upside-Down World of Wealth

Wait, you're not done yet. If you're a RUB right now, you're probably thinking that the giraffe thing was pretty idiotic—and certainly not an indicator of wealth potential. You're still clinging firmly to the laws that have governed your life and your work from the very beginning of your career. Well, I'm about to turn your world upside down some more . . . Ready?

The RUB Inside

We were all "idiots" when we were young children. Born with a natural curiosity, we loved to explore. We took the most direct path to whatever we wanted. We had no knowledge of fear or failure. We took pleasure in achieving successes, no matter how small. We looked forward to the little treats and hugs that accompanied every achievement, from our first wobbly step to our first word. Those early years were the "idiot" years.

And then something happened. To be precise, rules happened. Suddenly we were rewarded not for individual achievement but for conforming to an ever more elaborate set of social, behavioral, and academic rules. Exploring a winding path while the rest of the class marched neatly in twos on a class field trip became cause for a tongue-lashing. Playing in a distant neighborhood with unknown friends got us grounded. It wasn't long before we learned the world's lessons: Don't take risks. Don't do anything different. Stay close to home. Watch out for danger. Listen to your elders (and betters). All we heard was "No. Stop asking so many questions."

Most of us promised ourselves we'd "do our own thing" just as soon as we grew up, left home, graduated, got a job . . . whatever. But the reality is, those pesky rules just stuck with us through all the years of higher education and career building. We stayed on the straight path. We did what was expected. We obeyed. And what was our reward? Today we're **R**ight side **U**p and **B**roke—we're RUBs.

The good news is that deep inside every RUB is an "idiot"—a Rich Idiot—just waiting to get out. So don't worry. I'm giving you the key to unlock the prison door so you can set your inner Rich Idiot free.

Remember!
Often the kid who learns the most in school
is the one who's in the most trouble, because that
kid has to learn how to get out of it.

Wow, I Didn't Know That!

Are you ready to empty your mind and turn your old world upside down?

Maybe not. Maybe you're skeptical at this point. After all, you've already read a ton of self-help books on how to make money, but you're not rich yet, right? Probably not even close. Watch out! Hold on to your head—because I'm about to turn your wealth thinking upside down! You're going to start saying, "Wow, I didn't know that," and with every *Wow* you're going to get closer to your own wealth.

Remember!
Self-help doesn't work—duh!

Your first upside-down message is this: *Self*-help doesn't work. Got that? Let me repeat it. *Self*-help *doesn't work.*

Notice that the emphasis is on the *self*, not on the *help*.

Just think about it for a minute. If *self*-help worked, you would be wealthy by now, right? But you're not wealthy. So what did you do?

You went out and bought *this* book, thinking that it's another "how to get rich easily" self-help book.

That's what RUBs do. They keep on buying self-help books even though the evidence of their own bank account—or, rather, the *lack* of evidence in that account—shows them that a lot of what they've learned is not reducing their debt or increasing their wealth. What's the only thing that's happened? RUBs are suffering from caffeine deprivation because they're busy tossing change for designer coffee into a bank account, hoping that these few coins turn into a fortune. Or they're busy using up reams of paper making "Get Rich To-Do Lists" or they're sitting staring into space, trying to "attract" wealth through the magnetism of the cosmos.

Lucky you. You have in hand a book that's going to finally show you why all the things you have been doing all your life *aren't* working. The first thing is, you must unlearn the notion that self-help can turn you from the RUB you are into the Rich Idiot you aspire to be. And there's nothing wrong with that. There's no shame, only smarts, in admitting you simply don't get it. You don't know how to go from where you are to where you want to be. Like you, I love self-help books. I read them all the time. Many of the authors are my friends. But if self-help worked, everyone would be rich. So stop a minute and think about it. If you *could* have done it by yourself, you *would* have. If wishes and magnets and spare change were all you needed, you wouldn't be sitting there reading this book right now. The first big lightbulb that's going to illuminate your path is: Self-help doesn't work because we all need help. We've all been taught not to ask for help. So stop beating yourself up. Accept it. And move on.

Remember!
Rich is not a spectator sport. Rich is a team sport.

You need the power of Rich Idiot friends—and I'm going to be your first one.

This book will show you how to identify the players who will make up your wealth Dream Team. And it will show you how to cut the ones who are holding you back. You will learn how to quickly and easily locate mentors—wealth guides—who have already accomplished what you want to accomplish, and how to get them to point out the path to the summit. You'll learn how to tap into the ideas, the money, the time, and the talent of others to build your dream life. You will learn how valuable you are and how to become a rich friend and team member on a myriad of Rich Idiot teams. (Yes, you *will* be rich.)

Remember!
It's not only about the *M* in *money*,
it's also about the *T* in *time* and the *L* in *life*.

What is *rich* anyway? What does *rich* mean to you? Does it mean a bigger house? A better car? A bigger office? Designer clothes? Diamonds? A private plane? Guess what: If you mentioned any of these things, you don't quite "get it" yet. The house, the car, the clothes, the toys are all things you buy with money—but they aren't wealth. And the longer you cling to the idea that wealth is money, the longer you'll remain a RUB and the longer it will take you to become a Rich Idiot.

Before you begin to protest that you *want* all the toys—those status symbols of wealth—chill. You can have them. There's nothing wrong with that. In fact, many of these status symbols make life more pleasurable and comfortable.

Let's face it: Traveling first-class is preferable to being herded into the back of a plane with no leg room and served "plastic" munchies. Flying in your own jet is better still, since it means avoiding those long security lines and not having to show your toothpaste and meds to the entire traveling world.

Similarly, wearing clothes and shoes that fit well, are expertly crafted, and are made of the best materials is preferable to wearing cheap fabrics with stingy seams or stuffing your feet into man-made uppers instead of leather.

And who can deny that a Porsche or Ferrari offers a better ride than a more modestly priced car with a more conservative design?

I *want* you to have all those perks and toys, but then I want you to move on—because of a simple incontestable truth:

Real wealth is time. It's time to spend with your loved ones. Time to go on three-month vacations, like I do. Time to give back to those who have less.

Now, it's true that you can buy time with money and that the more money you have, the more time you can buy. But it's also true that to attract money you must have a wealth goal that isn't about money. Sounds like a contradiction, but it isn't. Having money won't make you a Rich Idiot. Having time will. Time to do what you want to do, when you want to do it, and with whom.

Think about it. Think what a kick it would be to have time to volunteer in your community and help others; to write a book; to chop down your own Christmas tree; to pick strawberries or apples with your kids; to visit a zoo. All without having to beg your boss for time off, or worry about the money you aren't earning in the hours you're doing something other than working.

Learn to work for time, not for money. By applying the seven secrets in this book you'll see how easily money comes when you make it to buy the time you want for your perfect life.

Remember!
If you think too much, you'll grow broke.

Be honest: Does the following describe you?

You overthink every opportunity. You love to analyze. You believe that by paying excruciatingly careful attention to every detail you're showing how smart you are. You examine everything that can go wrong. You spend hours studying every scrap of paper you can find. You build complex probability charts and graphs in pretty colors. You fill notebook after notebook with formulas for success. You keep those piles of T-shirts neatly folded. But by the time you pull the trigger (if you ever do), the opportunity you've studied so carefully has long since disappeared—most likely grabbed by a Rich Idiot.

Well, guess what? It's all because you think too much. That's why you're not a Rich Idiot.

There's another aspect to this. If you're a RUB, you've become too heavily invested in your own smartness. You resist shedding what you've learned and even balk at acquiring new information. After all, you're the one who burned the midnight oil; got the straight A's; attended all the lectures; and didn't skip a single class. After doing all that work, the RUB in you wants to hold on to what you've learned really tightly. Never let go. But your head is so full of old stuff there's no room for anything new. The result? RUBs like you are so rigid and set in your ways you can't easily accept new ideas that could rapidly accelerate your wealth acquisition.

Now, don't get me wrong: Rich Idiots *do* spend time thinking. But they don't spend a lot of time *learning*. Idiots seek only what they absolutely have to know or who they have to know to get rich—or richer. Because they haven't invested too much precious time, they don't get attached to what they've studied. They read books and newspapers, but they spend more time asking questions and adding Rich Idiots to their circle of friends. Because they're always searching for the next opportunity they *love* new information and quickly add it to what they know. Then they get rid of old information and ideas that may be past their sell-by dates.

Here are three ways Rich Idiots gather wealth-making knowledge:

- They get the basic facts. (I'm talking about a couple of pages of notes, max.)
- They check out those facts with people who've made money by taking advantage of a similar opportunity.
- They take the pulse of their own instincts, which they trust, and they focus on taking action.

Then they pull the trigger. Applying this strategy, a Rich Idiot can take advantage of four times the number of opportunities that the smart overthinker can.

Remember!
Love wealth or lose it.

RUBs are secret snobs who deep down inside think they're somehow better than Rich Idiots. You know I'm right. RUBs have a secret and deep-seated hostility toward the wealthy. They want wealth but don't want to *be* the wealthy. This dichotomy gets in the way of their ability to go flat out to become rich. Instead of attracting wealth, they repel it—sending out their mixed messages.

This "I want to be rich but I'm better than that" attitude prevails everywhere. Take the movie *Titanic*. Look at how the poor steerage passengers were portrayed—as sympathetic, honest, and totally likable. Contrast that with the traits attributed to the first-class passengers: cold, calculating, and unethical. We were supposed to be *glad* when they went down with the ship. If you carry this inner conflict around, it can be fatal to your acquisition of real wealth.

Rich Idiots, on the other hand, aspire to wealth. They want to be just like the wealthy people they see exalted in the media; they want to shop on Rodeo Drive. They want fine dining, good schools for their kids, beautiful homes in safe neighborhoods. They want to give their time and their money to worthwhile causes. They want to be in the company of other Rich Idiots. And because they have a strong desire and a clear goal, they reach wealth faster.

You have to make up your mind *right now* that it's okay to be rich. Not only is it okay but it's who you really are deep inside—rich. You have to believe that the entire universe—the grand design, if you will—calls for you to have abundance for yourself and to share with others.

Remember!
Rich Idiots send their money to work
while they stay home and play.

This is my favorite. RUBs believe they have to *work hard to get rich*. That's what you believe, too, right? You believe in the work ethic, in putting in the hours, in keeping your nose to the grindstone. And you do exactly that. When you don't work hard, you feel guilty. And you believe that somehow you don't deserve to have money that you don't work for 24/7, right?

Admit it: Isn't something like the following dialogue running through your head even as you're reading this? "That guy over there who made all that money from real estate—he's not really *rich*," you declare, "because all he really has is *money*. Why, I have much more. Heck, I enjoy the serene comfort of just collecting my paycheck every week. I don't have to spend every waking minute scanning for 'leads.' I don't have to be woken in the middle of the night by tenants wanting leaky faucets fixed. I don't have to deal with all that riffraff at foreclosure auctions or in those lousy neighborhoods he must go to in order to find plum properties. And my company gives me a nice health plan, a life insurance policy, and a retirement plan. Plus, I'm doing a job that challenges my brain—that impresses people." This same kind of dialogue rationalizes not playing the market or running a business: "Too much time . . . too much hassle . . . no safety net . . . not enough cachet."

Or what about this dialogue:

"I know my second cousin's best friend started that business selling pots and pans to her friends and neighbors and made a fortune, but she's not really *rich*. She has to organize those parties, deal with taking orders, deliveries, returns, and customers. She has to make herself available in the evenings, and she's putting miles on her car and minutes on her phone bill. I'm much better off working in the office with set hours, a guaranteed vacation, and benefits. Even if I need a part-time job so my kids can have some treats—so what, I'm happy to do it. My life is organized."

Not Rich Idiots. They don't believe in the classic work ethic. They don't believe in putting in hours of hard work. Quite the opposite. Rich Idiots don't want to spend time working; they want to spend time with their families. They want to participate in charitable organizations. They want to play. Rich Idiots want to send their money to work. And they do.

In fact, Rich Idiots have a whole different dialogue running through their heads than RUBs do. It goes something like this: "I added another property to my portfolio and handed it over to my professional management company. The deal I just put together was for a lease with an option to buy—which meant I got a great property with great tenants and they got a real chance to become home owners and start on their own path to real wealth—win-win all around."

Or how about this for more Rich Idiot self-speak: "I love the fact that I don't report to anyone . . . that I can take my kids to the park or to the movies in the afternoon . . . that my family and I aren't restricted to the two or three vacation weeks that companies offer their employees and we can take off for a month or two or even three months at a time . . . I feel secure that I'm dependent not on a single employer for my income but, rather, a collection of real estate, stocks and bonds, mutual funds, and my own business." The Rich Idiot has time, no hassles, a huge safety net, and plenty of cachet.

You will, too, by the time you've finished applying the secrets in this book. Because I'm going to teach you how to successfully take charge of your own financial life. I'll show you step by step how to free yourself from dependency on a company and a boss for your income and personal achievements. I'll show you how to find security in making your own decisions, in directing your own money, in being your own boss, in making your own investments.

I'll show you how to start, what to do, and how to find the people who can and will help you. I'll show you how to reduce your feelings of fear and risk while increasing your sense of real accomplishment, independence, and pride. I'll show you how to find time to spend with your loved ones, take multiple vacations, visit places you only dreamed about, live in the kind of home you see in magazines, drive your ultimate dream car, and dress for wealth. I'll help you be the generous, giving, caring, and sharing person you always wanted to be. I'll show you how to make your financial dreams come true.

All you have to do is turn your thinking upside down and let this Rich Idiot show you the way. Remember, the pot of gold at the end of the rainbow is at the bottom, not at the top!

And that's your Rich Idiot Secret No. 1.

Your Rich Idiot Upside-Down Action Plan

Follow this plan, starting now, to create the true wealth you desire.

1. Turn your own thinking upside down.

In a notebook write down as many things as you can about your true feelings, emotions, and attitudes toward money. Specifically, write down what scares you about making money. What do you think has stopped you from becoming wealthy in the past?

Now write down what you *wish* you felt about money. What would you do if you weren't so afraid?

Write down all your ideas about money that you need to turn upside down so wealth can come in.

2. Create your wealth wish list.

Make a list of all the things you would do if you had unlimited wealth. It doesn't matter how outrageous or seemingly impossible. It doesn't matter how many items you list. This is your private "wealth for life" list.

What would you do for your family, friends, and community? What kind of car would you drive? What kind of home would you have? What causes would you support?

Read that list every morning and every evening. And as each of your wealth wishes comes true, cross it off and add others.

3. Get a wealth talisman or wealth charm.

Rich Idiots have wealth talismans or charms with them at all times. These don't make you rich, but they do remind you to focus your energy and your thoughts on becoming a Rich Idiot. Kind of like the string you tie around your finger. Talismans come in many shapes and sizes. Mine is a silver bracelet I wear on my wrist every day. It's inscribed with my own secret wealth message. Every time I look at it I am reminded of my wealth goal and also of all the riches I already have. You need to have a talisman, too. It can be a bracelet or one of the semiprecious stones, like jade, that's associated with abundance and riches, or even just a simple string around your finger. Check out my Web site www.GetRichWithRobert.com for more ideas.

secret no. 2

Follow the Spiritual Laws of Wealth

See the invisible.
Feel the intangible.
Achieve the impossible.
— ANONYMOUS

Warning!
If you're not religious or spiritual and don't believe,
or if you just refuse to consider spirituality a valid thing to
write about in a book on wealth, don't read this chapter.

If you are religious or spiritual,
please feel free to rely on your own beliefs.
But you should know that most of the spiritual
laws I advocate are general in nature, equally applicable
whether you refer in your beliefs to God, Jesus,
Muhammad, Buddha, Light, Energy, or the Universe.

Many Rich Idiots know with certainty that
these spiritual laws govern their wealth.

Spiritual Laws of Wealth

What's that? you say. You didn't know there are spiritual laws governing wealth?

There are. And they're unexpectedly powerful. Break them and risk staying broke. Adhere to them and let abundance flow to you.

In the previous chapter you learned that to be a Rich Idiot you've got to turn your *thinking* upside down. In this chapter you'll learn about turning your *believing* upside down.

Why? Because wealth is governed by two sets of laws: There are the physical laws of money, but there are also the spiritual laws.

Most Rich Idiots believe in both and follow them.

I'm not going to kid you. You already know that Rich Idiots don't get rich all by themselves. They have friends. They have mentors. They have guides. They have helpers. Rich Idiots tap into the power of others. Rich Idiots get help. You understand that.

But here's another amazing, upside-down secret. Rich Idiots also tap into the power of . . . well, let's just call it the "Universe." Rich Idiots don't just depend on physical or human resources to reach their goals; Rich Idiots depend on spiritual resources.

Remember!
Turn your beliefs upside down.

Most Rich Idiots believe in the spiritual laws of wealth. Not only do they believe in them, they follow them to the letter. Why? Because Rich Idiots know something RUBs don't know. Rich Idiots know that when it comes to building wealth, spiritual laws trump physical laws every time. Believe this. Every dollar that comes to you journeys through a Universe of wealth that's as old as the world itself.

Right about now, some of you are probably ready to skip this chapter. You're saying to yourself, "This is a little too woo-woo for me." Or maybe you're thinking, "I'm already a person of faith, so I don't have to read this." Maybe even a few of you are downright incensed. "Where does this guy get off?" you're thinking. "I bought this book to find out how to get rich, not read a sermon."

Let me assure you, the concepts I'm about to present cross all religious lines. They apply to the most devout as well as the most cynical, and I attribute much of my own success to following the laws I'm going to share with you now.

Plus, I have some impressive people seconding my opinion.

For example, Ralph Waldo Emerson, one of the great thinkers of the nineteenth century, wrote, in "The Progress of Culture," "Great men are they who see that spiritual is stronger than any material force."

Deepak Chopra, a best-selling author and spiritual guide to millions, says, "Human beings are made of body, mind and spirit. Of these spirit is primary, for it connects us to the source of everything." And that includes wealth.

Randy Gage, the author of *Accept Your Abundance: Why You Are Supposed to Be Wealthy*, writes,

> I believe that money is . . . the Universe in action. There's no separation. Sunshine and full moons and walks on the beach are spiritual. Good health, happy relationships and love are spiritual too. But so are financial security, a nice home, beautiful clothes and a car that makes your heart race! Because the only way you get and keep the material things is by giving a fair exchange of value, and living the spiritual laws of prosperity.

Those Mystery Money Moments

We've all had this experience: You've reached the end of your financial rope. You're about to go under. You've exhausted every financial resource you can think of when suddenly, from out of the blue, comes the exact amount of money that will save you! This is the mystery money moment that Squire Rushnell writes about in his book *When God Winks*.

> . . . A widow was having a hard time. Her husband's life insurance proceeds had run out, and she couldn't get a job. Her teenagers were growing out of their clothes and the cupboard was bare. One morning she assessed her situation. The rent was overdue for $550. Her electricity would be shut off unless she paid $44. The phone company was breathing down her neck for a payment of $31. That meant she needed $625. Her checkbook showed a balance of $24. . . . Before she went into town to run some errands, she took her Bible from the shelf, placed it on the floor, and stood on it. "Lord, you've said to stand on your word and you'll supply all our needs. Well, here I am." Then she stepped down off her Bible and went on her way. At the post office her heart leapt. Two letters fell from the junk mail. One held a $310 residual check from an old commercial she had no idea was still running; the other, a $75 refund from a college to which her son had applied. Buoyant with renewed hope, she rushed to deposit the checks at the bank. That's when she received another joyful piece of news; there had been a clerical error—her checkbook balance was not $24, it was $240! After the deposits, her bank balance stood at $625—the exact amount she needed to pay the rent and the electric and phone bills.

Sure, stories like that sound too born-to-be-a-parable to be true, but I've had enough similar experiences to take this account as true.

There are thousands of mystery money moments that just can't be explained by the material laws of wealth alone.

The generosity of the Universe doesn't always come in the form of actual cash money—sometimes it comes in other surprising forms.

Did a person ever come into your life and change it at the exact moment it needed changing? Did you ever get a career break at the exact moment you needed one? Did you ever experience a rebirth—spiritual, ethical, or moral—that brought you riches you never expected? Have you ever noticed that when you're just about at the end of your financial resources—broke—just enough money comes in to keep you going?

All those events and moments that we think of as coincidence or luck are really the Universe touching our lives and helping us, or turning us to a more favorable life path.

Trust those moments.

Spiritual Wealth Quiz

Respecting the spiritual laws of wealth is a major part of becoming a Rich Idiot. To find out exactly where you fit on the spiritual wealth scale take this quiz.

1. There are spiritual laws that govern wealth.
   a) I believe that.
   b) I'm not sure I believe that.
   c) I don't believe that at all.

2. Rich people are greedy and selfish.
   a) I believe that all rich people are greedy—they must be to have grabbed so much.
   b) I believe that rich people are like the rest of us—greedy sometimes, generous other times.
   c) I believe that, compared with the general population, rich people are less greedy and more generous and unselfish.

3. The Universe is an abundant place and there's more than enough for everyone.

a) I believe we live in a world of scarcity and that if one person gets a big slice of the pie, another winds up in need.

b) I agree that the Universe is an abundant place and that there's more than enough for everyone.

c) I believe that the Universe favors some people over others and distributes wealth unevenly.

4. Which of these statements best describes your feelings?

a) I get so jealous when I see someone with a bigger house, a better car, nicer clothes, and a life with no worries, while I'm struggling to pay the bills and keep a roof over my family's heads.

b) I love meeting wealthy and successful people because it proves that wealth is out there, and if those Rich Idiots can do it, so can I.

5. I think there's something inside me stopping me from being rich. I guess I don't really deserve to be rich and should just be happy with what I have.

a) I believe this statement to be true.

b) I don't agree with this statement, though I'm not exactly sure yet how to get on the path to riches.

Spiritual Wealth Quiz Scoring

Ready? Let's see how you did. Let's see if you're still in RUB mode—thinking **R**ight side **U**p and **B**roke—or if you've developed the mindset of a Rich Idiot.

1. There are spiritual laws that govern wealth.

If you answered a), "I believe that," give yourself a pat on the back. You've entered the zone where most Rich Idiots and their money reside.

If you answered b), "I'm not sure I believe that," get off the fence, or put the spiritual laws to a test. Go ahead. How much do you really need right now? Ask for it. And see what happens.

If you answered c), "I don't believe that at all," you can still make money. You can still get rich, sort of. But you'll never enjoy the blessings of true abundance that the Universe can pour into your life. You may possess money but you'll find it won't make you a Rich Idiot. You'll remain a RUB.

2. Rich people are greedy and selfish.

If you answered a), "I believe that all rich people are greedy—they must be to have grabbed so much," you're thinking like a real RUB. Your image of the wealthy as greedy and grasping is wrong, and it will block your path to Rich Idiot status. The reality is, Rich Idiots aren't greedy. You don't believe me? Believe this: A study conducted by the Spectrum Group in 2004 found that households with $500,000 or more in assets gave away 6 percent of their income, while those with a net worth of $5 million or more contributed 6.1 percent to various charitable causes. This compares with an average of 2 percent for all American households (read: RUBs). So much for the "greedy" Rich Idiot image. Banish that right now.

If you answered b), "I believe that rich people are like the rest of us—greedy sometimes, generous other times," go back and read the paragraph above. Statistics don't lie. The fact is that, overall, Rich Idiots are *more* generous than the rest of the population—RUBs included.

If you answered c), "I believe that, compared with the general population, rich people are less greedy and more generous and unselfish," you've shown that your spirit is that of a true Rich Idiot. You're on the fast track to where you want to be. Why do I say that? Because since you believe that the wealthy are generous and giving, you've no unresolved inner conflicts about becoming wealthy, too. In contrast, RUBs who believe it's somehow evil to be rich are encumbered by conflicting messages. How can the Universe send you wealth, riches, and abundance when you've set up spiritual barriers to block them?

3. The Universe is an abundant place and there's more than enough for everyone.

If you answered a), "I believe we live in a world of scarcity and that if one person gets a big slice of the pie, another ends up in need," you have a scarcity spirit. You don't believe in the abundance of the Universe. You believe that if your neighbor acquires more wealth, that leaves less for you. Not true. Universal wealth bubbles up from a spring that has no bottom and can never be emptied. Lose this type of thinking right away because it will seriously hurt your chances of becoming a Rich Idiot. In fact, I'll go so far as to say that abundance for all is one of the fundamental principles of the Universe. "May God give you of the dew of heaven, and the fatness of the earth, and plenty of grain and wine," reads the blessing of Isaac in Genesis 27:28. "Every blade of grass has its Angel that bends over it and whispers, 'Grow—grow!'" teaches the Talmud. Or consider this, from Midrash Exodus Rabbah 31:12: "There is nothing in the world more grievous than poverty."

If you answered b), "I agree that the Universe is an abundant place and that there's more than enough for everyone," congratulations! You've got the Rich Idiot abundance mentality. In believing that there's plenty out there, you've opened yourself to letting it flow to you.

If you answered c), "I believe that the Universe favors some people over others and distributes wealth unevenly," your belief system is that of a RUB. Get over it.

4. Which of these statements best describes your feelings?

If you answered a), "I get so jealous when I see someone with a bigger house, a better car, nicer clothes, and a life with no worries, while I'm struggling to pay the bills and keep a roof over my family's heads," you're firmly in RUB-land. This jealousy is very detrimental to the acquisition of riches. If you see a wealthy person and think, "They don't deserve it" or "What a waste" or "That's stupid," those are unfounded, deeply negative thoughts. You're casting what is called the evil eye. The Universe and the world of money reflect back what you send out. So every time you say or think, "They don't deserve it," what's coming back to you from the Universe is "*You* don't deserve it." Your thoughts are boomerangs. They will always come right back to you. Rich Idiots know that, and because they know it they celebrate the success of other Rich Idiots. They make the wealthy their friends. They send thanks to the Universe for the good fortune of others, knowing that their joy in others' wealth will result in their own wealth. Get rid of the sour grapes. They're spoiling your wealth harvest potential. Remember, negative people who convey their blame or accuse you or others are usually just talking about themselves: cheaters accuse others of cheating, liars accuse others of lying.

If you answered b), "I love meeting wealthy and successful people because it proves that wealth is out there, and if those Rich Idiots can do it, so can I," good for you. Step up to the front of the Rich Idiot line.

5. I think there's something inside me stopping me from being rich. I guess I don't really deserve to be rich and should just be happy with what I have.

If you answered a), "I believe this statement to be true," you're in a dangerous, undeserving place. The Universe is very smart. It not only sends you what you ask for directly, it monitors what you're saying indirectly. This statement says, "I'm not worthy, so go right on past and give all the wealth to someone else." The Universe doesn't want you to just "settle." There's a full, rich life waiting for you to enjoy and share. Go out and get it. Stop thinking you don't deserve it. You do.

If you answered b), "I don't agree with this statement, though I'm not exactly sure yet how to get on the path to riches," I think you just have to go on faith. One of the hardest things about wealth is wanting it! You've got to want wealth or you won't get any. You also have to believe you deserve wealth or you won't get any. You've got to believe in yourself. You've got to believe in what I'm telling you. Try it. The only thing you have to lose is your inner RUB.

Rich Idiot	vs.	RUB
The Universe helps me	vs.	The Universe is just more blah blah
Desire is good	vs.	Desire is bad
Abundance	vs.	Scarcity
Happiness for wealth of others	vs.	Envy at wealth of others
I deserve it all	vs.	I'm not worthy

Spiritual Wealth Prep

Before I can reveal the two fundamental spiritual laws of wealth that are going to turn your belief upside down, let's get you prepped. I want you to clear out old, rusty ways of relating to yourself, others, and the Universe. Let's get you all scrubbed and shiny like a Rich Idiot.

Your Rich Idiot spiritual wealth prep consists of two simple steps:

- Forgive
- Commit

Forgive

The first thing you have to do is to forgive. "But I'm not holding any grudges," you protest. Give me a break. Let's do a quick checklist of possible forgiveness targets. Can you tell me that one or more of these groups hasn't ever made you angry or jealous? Hasn't ever disappointed you or betrayed you? Hasn't hurt you or frightened you? Of course, one or more of them have. So the first thing we're going to do is forgive.

- Forgive your parents.
- Forgive your siblings.
- Forgive your spouse.
- Forgive your kids.
- Forgive other members of your family.
- Forgive friends who let you down.
- Forgive your coworkers.
- Forgive your neighbors.
- Forgive people you come in contact with daily.

Forgiveness is the first step to cleaning out old "stuff" and making room for new wealth to come pouring in. Forgiveness isn't something you do once a week. Forgiveness is a daily cleanser, preparing your spirit for the riches to come. "Keeping score of old scores and scars, getting even and one-upping, always make you less than you are," said Malcolm Forbes, one of the most wealthy and successful Rich Idiots.

But our list isn't complete. One of the most important acts of forgiveness is forgiving yourself. It's a balm. It soothes. It heals. It prepares you for access to those spiritual laws of wealth that can change not only your life but the lives of all you touch.

Remember!
To err is human. To forgive can make you rich.

Your Forgiveness Scripts
I wrote this forgiveness script for myself. I fill it out and say it at least once a week. It helps me align my energy with the goodness of the

Universe rather than diverting it to revenge or other toxic, energy-draining emotions.

Forgiveness Script 1

(This script is for you to say to yourself to forgive others.)

I forgive you, _____ [insert the name of the person you're forgiving], for anything you've done to me in the past, anything you may be doing to me in the present, and whatever you may do to me in the future. I forgive you now completely.

Forgiveness Script 2

(This script is for you to say to yourself when you believe you need forgiveness for what you may have done against another.)

Please, _____ [insert a name], forgive me for anything I may have done in the past, am doing in the present, or will do in the future. Please forgive me now.

Forgiveness Script 3

(This script is the universal act of forgiveness you bestow on yourself.)

I now forgive myself completely for _____ [insert what you're forgiving yourself for here].

Warning!

Forgiveness does not absolve you from the responsibility of wrongs you have committed. One must always be responsible and held responsible for any wrongs they have done. Forgiveness is a separate act.

Commit

This is a very important part of your Rich Idiot prep. What it means is this: First, you must acknowledge that if you're not a Rich Idiot yet, you haven't been committed to becoming one. This is tough. This is accepting full responsibility for your lack of wealth. This is no excuses, no passing the buck, no "yeah but's." This is you standing up and admitting that you're not a Rich Idiot because you weren't committed fully to wealth.

The second part of this prep is to now commit to wealth. Want it. Believe it. Take responsibility for bringing it into your life.

Let me tell you a story about something that happened to me many years ago. I had no money and no cash in the bank. To tell you the absolute truth, I was broke. I couldn't pay my bills. I was stressed out. I thought about nothing else day and night, week after week, month after month. It was a really tough time for me. Some of you have been there, right? Some of you may be there now. The bottom line is, we've *all* been there.

One day a wealthy friend of mine said, "Robert, I'm noticing that you're not your usual happy self. You seem to be going through a rough patch." I was so relieved that someone had noticed and maybe was going to help that I admitted my feelings. "Absolutely," I said. "I'm so stressed out. I don't have enough money. I can't pay the bills. I can't save anything. My money life is week to week, and sometimes it's even day to day. I don't know what's going to happen. I'm scared. And I feel really poor right now."

Remember!
Rich or poor—what you've got is what you want.

Instead of sympathy, here's what I got from him: "Robert, whatever you're experiencing now—being broke and stressed—that's what you're committed to. Underline *committed*."

"What do you mean?" I shot back.

"Well, you're obviously committed to being stressed out, living broke, and being poor."

I couldn't believe it. "Are you kidding?" I responded, ang
even more frustrated. "I *want* to be rich. I *want* to have plenty of
money. I *want* to take care of my family. I *want* to be able to give to
others. But I'm broke! Don't you get it? I'm broke!" I was practically
shouting, arguing with him, getting more frustrated and defensive by
the minute.

And then I shut up, took a deep breath, and started to really listen
to what he was saying. "If you smoke cigarettes and don't quit, no matter how many times you say you'll try, your commitment is to smok-
ing," he explained calmly. "If you're poor, then on some level you're
committed to being poor. Change the commitment and you'll change
the result. Commit to being rich and happy. And the minute you commit, those things will come into your life."

This was his way of telling me to allow the Universe to come into
my spirit by preparing my spirit to receive wealth. To commit to a new
result!

Your Commit Script

Here's a script that will help you commit to a wealth result. Say
the words twice a day: once before you begin your day, then again at
bedtime. Say the words with feeling and in the belief that you're now
committed to a new and better personal financial outcome and *will*
get it.

I'm _____ *[say your name here]. This is my commitment:*

    I commit to filling my life with wealth.
    I commit to filling my life with happiness.
    I commit to being bold.
    I commit to taking positive actions.
    I commit to a new result.

    Now you're ready.

The Two Spiritual Laws of Wealth

Law No. 1   Get.

Law No. 2   Give.

The First Spiritual Law of Wealth

Practically every book out there that addresses the spiritual laws of wealth begins with this profound command: Give to get.

Not the Rich Idiot. In the upside-down spiritual world of Rich Idiots, the primary directive is very different. The number one spiritual law of wealth in the Rich Idiot's universe is the exact opposite: *Get* to *give.* This law is the most difficult one for RUBs to come to terms with. Think I'm kidding? Take the following quiz and find out whether you're thinking Rich Idiot or RUB when it comes to getting.

Remember!
The more you get, the more you can give.

Spiritual Quiz

You're at my wealth-creating seminar. All around you are thousands of other Rich Idiots in training. Suddenly I interrupt my presentation and pull out ten one-hundred-dollar bills. I wave them above my head and ask, "Who wants one of these hundred-dollar bills? Come on up."

What do you do?

1. Keep your butt firmly in your seat.
2. Wait until someone else goes up and only then go up, too.
3. Decide that it's a perfect moment for a cup of coffee, a trip to the john, a cigarette break—anything so you can get out of there and not be involved in the money-giveaway game.
4. Run right up.

You just ran out to pick up a couple of things from the grocery store. To your horror, as the cashier rings up your purchases you realize you forgot your wallet. A search through your pockets yields $4.67. You're short 97 cents. Suddenly, the person behind you in line takes out a dollar and hands it to you.

What do you do?

1. Mumble something that sounds suspiciously like "Thanks but no thanks," slink off to replace all your items, and leave the store as fast as possible.
2. Start figuring out which of the items you can do without, so you can cover the cost of the groceries with your own cash.
3. Say thank you very politely, take the money, pay for the groceries, and go home, blessing the kindness of strangers.

You're on your way to a very important appointment—a job interview, a hot date, your kid's first solo violin recital, whatever. You get a flat tire. Worse, you forgot to recharge your cell phone and now you have no way of calling to get the tire fixed or explain your delay. A total stranger walks by, sees you struggling, and offers you her cell phone.

What do you do?

1. Say "No thanks," get right back into your car, and sit there telling yourself how stupid you are while also fuming at your wife, your kid, the phone company, your life, the Universe.
2. Say "No thanks" and start walking in search of a pay phone.
3. Accept the offer of the cell phone with thanks. Make your calls.

You're struggling with a project at work that's just not coming together. One of your colleagues steps up to the plate and offers to help. What do you do?

1. Deny and decline. Deny that you're having trouble and decline any offer of help.
2. Say a polite thank-you, then spend the next two weeks stressing about what you imagine was a plot your colleague cooked up to make you look stupid in front of your boss so she could get you fired and step into your position.
3. Accept the offer of help with gratitude.

This is turning out to be one of those nightmarish mornings. You have a major (unfinished) paper due for your computer class tonight. It's your day to drive the car pool. You forgot your promise to bake four dozen cupcakes for your daughter's Brownie troop. Your other daughter won't leave the house without her favorite socks. The dryer just made that funny noise again and gave out. All the laundry, including the "I won't leave home without my favorite" socks, is a soggy mess. Your toddler has soiled himself for the second time. You're seven months pregnant. It has started to snow—big-time. And to top it all off, your spouse left last night for a three-day business conference on some tropical island. The doorbell rings. It's your mother-in-law. She's got her suitcase and is offering to stay for a couple of days to help.

What do you do?

1. Go bright red with embarrassment that she's caught you off guard with a domestic disaster and kick yourself for being such a failure at everything. Thank her. Insist that you're fine and all is well. Tell her you'll call and hustle her out the door as fast as possible.
2. Start picking up the mess and apologizing for everything as you follow her through the disaster and into the kitchen. Promise that you'll only need her for an hour, at the most. Beg her not to "touch a thing." Assure her that everything is under control and that this is *not* a normal morning.
3. Give her a huge smile and a hug of gratitude. Grab your class assignment, the car keys, and your Starbucks card and leave her to deal with the kids, the dryer, the socks, and the poop.

What did you pick?

Did you run up for the $100?

Did you pay for your groceries with a stranger's money?

Did you accept the offer of a cell phone?

Did you welcome the gift of help from your mother-in-law?

If these were not your answers, you're a RUB—**R**ight side **U**p and **B**roke—because by *not* accepting these gifts you've broken the first spiritual law of Rich Idiots. Again, that's the law of receiving abundance with gratitude—the law of "get."

Your Spiritual Wealth Makeover

I know: We've all been programmed to believe we have to give in order to receive. Givers are better than getters.

But here's the upside-down part that Rich Idiots understand. Getting comes first. It has to. Like putting an airplane oxygen mask on your own face first before you can help your toddler with his, you have to first *receive* the gifts of abundance *before* you can give them. I know that most of us are uncomfortable with receiving. We feel unworthy, guilty, obligated, selfish . . . all the negatives. If I suddenly jumped out of this book and gave you $1,000 you might think, "What's the catch?" or "Why's he giving it to me?" You'd be uncomfortable about receiving.

But Rich Idiots think of getting in a very different way. Rich Idiots know that the more they have, the more they can give. In fact, Rich Idiots crank this thinking up a notch and believe it's their duty to get more so they can give more.

Let me put it into dollar amounts.

You're stopped at a red light and a homeless man comes up and taps on your window. He's carrying a sign that says, "Vet. Sick. Homeless." You've just paid all your bills, and since you're living paycheck to paycheck you're not going to get any more money until tomorrow. All you've got is $10.84 in your pocket. But you really want to help. You give him a dollar. Good for you. That's great. You've just given away almost 10 percent of what you've got. The Universe smiles down on you. But let's face it: One dollar doesn't go very far in helping a man who's sick and alone on the streets, with no home to shelter him.

Now, how about this:

You've finished this book. You're a few months into your own Rich Idiot program. You've built up your net worth so that it's now $100,000. You still really want to help people. You write a check to a local homeless shelter for $10,000—one-tenth of what you've got. This $10,000 will feed and shelter many suffering souls for a month!

Which was better? The dollar gift or the $10,000 gift?

How about this scenario:

You've arrived. You're a Mega-Rich Idiot, with a net worth of $10 million. But inside you're still the same person. The money hasn't changed the fact that you want to help others. So what do you do? You take $1 million (still only 10 percent of your wealth) and build a facility that can feed and shelter many people for a year, plus clothe them, provide them with medical attention, retrain them, and help them to become self-sufficient.

Which of these giving scenarios yields the best outcome?

You get the picture. Rich Idiots always want more so they can give more.

It's like Oprah says: "What material success does is provide you with the ability to concentrate on other things that really matter. And that is being able to make a difference, not only in your own life, but in other people's lives."

Patrons, Benefactors, and Saints

Mother Teresa

I know. Some of you are still skeptical. All that learning about "giving" is hard to unlearn. It's hard to view getting enormous wealth as a law—much like other laws. It's hard to imagine how getting can make you a bigger giver—more generous and able to help more people.

Try this. Think Mother Teresa. We all know her as a saint, as a woman who managed to inspire not just a nation but the entire world. Mother Teresa took up the vow of poverty. We never think of the money she needed and raised to accomplish her work. But she wasn't a stranger to the first spiritual law of wealth—the getting law. Quite the contrary: She managed to "get" (receive) millions of dollars so she could give help to thousands of poor and dying souls. This excerpt from *Frontline*, a current-affairs magazine in India, drives that point home.

> "Money," she [Mother Teresa] told her biographer, "I never give it a thought. It always comes." There are no estimates of the volume of donations to the congregation today, but the donations are known to run to millions of dollars.

Here was a saint who understood about money and receiving it. She understood the first spiritual law of wealth: Get.

Artists Get

For centuries, patrons used their massive wealth to support the arts and sciences. What if Michelangelo, Leonardo da Vinci, Shakespeare, Mozart, or Beethoven had decided they wouldn't take, receive, or otherwise open themselves to "get"? They wouldn't have been able to give the world some of the most beautiful memorials to the human spirit.

How to "Get" More

There are two keys that open the "get more" Universe:

1. The first is saying "Thank you" for what you have.
2. The second is asking for more.

Gratitude

Truisms about the power of gratitude in unlocking abundance range from a saying from the Hausa people of Nigeria—"Give thanks for a little and you'll find a lot"—to this strong testimonial from author Sarah Ban Breathnach: "Both abundance and lack exist simultaneously in our lives, as parallel realities. It is always our conscious choice which secret garden we will tend. . . . When we choose not to focus on what is missing from our lives but are grateful for the abundance that's present—love, health, family, friends, work, the joys of nature and personal pursuits that bring us pleasure—the wasteland of illusion falls away and we experience Heaven on earth."

If you want more money, if you're feeling impoverished, if you're feeling stressed out, you're not coming to abundance from the right place. The way to turn those feelings around and restore positive energy and flow is to simply say "Thank you." Be grateful for what you have because if you're not grateful for what the Universe has already given you, it's probably not going to give you any more.

Keep firmly in mind that there are people on the planet who don't have food, who don't have medicine, who don't have water. There are people who don't have children, or a family. There are people who don't have a girlfriend or a boyfriend or a husband or a wife. There are people who don't have a job and would be grateful for one. There are people who have to walk because they don't have a car. Now contrast that with what you have—and say "Thank you" for everything, no matter how large or how small.

Did you know that nearly one billion people entered the twenty-first century unable to read a book or even sign their name? Or that half the world—three billion people—live on less than $2 a day?!

I could hit you with pages of similarly devastating statistics, but then you'd be saying, "Come on, Robert, that's enough. I want you to show me how to make some more money and get where I want to go." So let's leave it at this: To build wealth you must first build positive energy by appreciating the real abundance you enjoy, then use that energy to begin energizing your finances and your fortune.

The Thank-You Note

Try this. I started to do it many years ago and have kept it up. Almost every time I pay a bill, I write a little thank-you on the check. When I pay the electric bill I send the power company a thank-you. When I pay the phone bill I send the phone company a thank-you. "Why would you do that?" I'm asked all the time. The answer is because every time I make even a small gesture like that the Universe rewards me for my thanks, sometimes in amounts that are extraordinary.

Remember!
For every bill you pay or check you write,
add a thank-you.

Ask

One of the most powerful affirmations of the gifts that are simply waiting for you is found in the New Testament (Luke 11:9–10): "And I say unto you, Ask, and it shall be given you; seek, and ye shall find; knock, and it shall be opened unto you. For every one that asketh receiveth; and he that seeketh findeth; and to him that knocked it shall be opened." What a powerful promise. And all you have to do is ask. Try it.

Ask Right

Give yourself permission to ask. Remember, Rich Idiots always ask for everything. They ask for help, for advice, for money. Get into the Rich Idiot asking mode.

Ask for what you want, not for what you don't want. A RUB would ask, "Please stop the bills from piling up," or "Please help me not to be broke." This is wrong asking. This asking attracts "bills" and "the state of being broke." Try this: "Please give me $1,000" or "Please give me prosperity." The difference in what you get will amaze you.

Add lots of details. Create a movie in your imagination of exactly what it is you want. Add as much detail as you can. Really "see" what you want the Universe to give you.

Ask the person who can grant your request. Don't waste your time asking people who don't have the authority or the power to grant your request. Go right up to the top, then ask.

That's it. That's the first spiritual law of wealth: Get. Now let's go to the second powerful law of wealth: Give—or, rather, give to get.

The Second Spiritual Law of Wealth

This is the law that we are most familiar with, because it's been drilled into us from childhood. "Give Johnny your truck," we've been told, or "Give Suzie your Barbie doll."

We've heard the "It's more blessed to give than to receive" statement—usually followed by the "Give and it shall be given unto you" promise—so many times that it's firmly rooted in our belief system. And there's great truth in this law. But for this law to bring you the abundance of the Universe you've got to know *how* to give. So here are Robert's Rules for giving (so that you'll be sure to receive).

The "I've Got Nothing to Give" Excuse

Before we begin, let's deal with the usual RUB whine: "But, Robert, I'm broke. I've got nothing to give." My response is: "Wrong. You've got lots to give. Let's make a list."

1. *Give a smile—duh*. Everyone's got one of those to give, and you can't imagine how one smile can lift a person's spirit; this often works for both the person giving it and the person receiving it. What are you waiting for? Put down the book and go smile at someone.

2. *Give thanks*. We've already talked about the power of thanks and gratitude in attracting wealth. Start right now. You can thank your second-grade teacher, who taught you how to read, thus making it possible for you to learn the seven secrets this book contains. Get up and pour yourself a glass of water. Now thank all the people who made that water safe and pure for you to drink. Write a couple of thank-you notes to people who have helped you. You get the idea.

3. *Give a hand*. Look around. Does someone need a hand? Can you carry a bag of groceries for someone who's older or infirm? Can you pick up that wrapper someone dropped in the street, giving a hand to the city workers who are keeping your town clean? Can you give your spouse a hand with dinner? Your kid a hand with his homework? The neighbor a hand with yard trash? Look around. I bet there are at least a dozen people you could give a hand to right now.

4. *Give a hug*. This is a big one. When was the last time you hugged someone you loved just "because"?

5. *Give an hour*. Okay, how much do you make an hour? Whatever it is, donate an hour of your time to a local cause. Read to patients in the hospital. Deliver meals to shut-ins. Volunteer at a shelter. Answer a help line. Congratulations—you've just given $5 or $10 or $100 or even $300. Who says you've got nothing to give?

The Positive Flow of Giving

I want to tell you a true story about something that happened to me. There are two points this story makes.

The first point is this: It's not the amount you give but how big that amount is relative to all that *you* have. If you have only $5 and you give $2.50, you have given one-half of your entire wealth. The Universe sees this as an enormous act of giving and rewards the giver hugely. Contrast this with the person who has $10 million and gives $1,000. The Universe sees this as cheap and withholding and in turn withholds additional abundance.

The second point is: Giving *always* results in getting.

Now back to my story and the spiritual guide who demonstrated the power of these two points.

I was asked by a friend of mine—a wise spiritual guide—to make a contribution to a charity. He also wanted to teach me about giving. I love to help, so I sat down and wrote him what I thought was a pretty generous check.

He looked at it. Looked at me. And then he tore it up. "Robert," he said, "I want you to write me another check. Only this time double the amount, so you can really feel it."

Well, I must admit I was a little taken aback, but I went ahead and wrote the check. And what did he do?

He tore that one up, too. "Robert," he said, "I want you to write me another check, and double it again."

Well, now I thought he was really pushing the envelope of charity and friendship. This was a huge amount of money he was asking for. This third check was going to really hurt. In fact, it would more than wipe out my available cash balance. But I've trusted this man for a long time, so I wrote the third check. But in handing it to him, I said, "Please don't deposit it for thirty days, because I won't have the funds until then to cover it."

He took the check without a word and left.

The next day he phoned and told me, "Robert, I deposited that generous check you just gave me in the bank and I'm calling to say thank you."

I couldn't believe it. I didn't have nearly enough money in the account. The check was going to bounce. Just as I was about to express my concern, my assistant came in with the mail. There were two envelopes. One was from a man I hadn't heard from in over seven years. I'd loaned him some money and he'd never repaid it until that moment—with interest! And the amount was more than I needed to cover that "ginormous" check.

But my story doesn't end there. There was a second envelope in the mail that day. It also contained a check—a huge check—for more than the one I'd written.

I'd given until it hurt. Until I was scared. And the Universe gave it back to me—double! That's the power of giving to get.

The Proper Giving

"Is there a right way to give, Robert?" I get asked all the time. "How do I know who to give to or where to give?" is another question I hear a lot.

"Yes. There's a proper way to give," I always answer. "And that's to give to something bigger than yourself." Everyone who is truly happy, truly wealthy, truly successful is committed to something bigger than themselves. If all you're committed to is yourself and making more money to buy more cars, clothes, and toys, you'll have a good time, but you'll come up empty—spiritually empty. And chances are the Universe isn't going to fill you up again.

Something along those lines happened to me. I made a ton of money. I took a whole year off. I did what everyone dreams of doing. And let me be very clear about this: I had a blast. All I did was go to beach resorts, travel the world, stay in unbelievable hotels, gamble a lot in casinos. And I kept buying things. Wherever I went. Whatever I saw. Whatever I wanted. I just bought it. I bought, and bought, and bought. Toys. Toys. Toys. Fun. Fun. Fun.

But then something happened to me. I was doing what everyone dreams of doing. I felt rich. I felt spoiled.

I was living everyone's dream, right? It's the "if only I won the lottery" dream. But it wasn't enough.

So what did my year teach me? It taught me that every relationship, even the relationship you'll have with your wealth when it begins to roll in, goes through three stages:

Stage One is the infatuation stage. You love it. It's exciting. It's a thrill. It's also an illusion. It's not sustainable. It can't last, and it never does.

Stage Two is the engagement stage. This is where you begin to settle down and think about spending your life with a certain special person, or with the wealth you're accumulating. This is the stage where you start to make commitments, but most people have fear and quit. They then go and seek out infatuation in stage one.

Stage Three is the commitment stage. This is where real Rich Idiots end up. This is where they commit to something bigger than themselves and their own immediate loved one. This is the real giving place—giving to charity, to your community, to your country, even to the world. When you reach this level, the excitement and infatuation come back to your relationships, work, and life forever.

So when I wrote this book, just as when I wrote my previous books, I didn't say, "Gee, I can't wait to sell a bunch of these books so I can rake in all those royalties." No. And when I give speeches, I don't say, "I just want to make this speech, collect my check, and get out of here." No.

I'm committed to something bigger than myself. I want to help people just like you earn enough money to make *your* dreams come true—and I do. I want to contribute to my community—and I do. I want to contribute to my country—and I do. I want to contribute to the world—and I do.

And that's the best part of being a Rich Idiot and following the second spiritual law of wealth: Give to get.

A Final Word About the Spiritual Laws of Wealth

You have to believe in them. It's as simple as that. Because you never really know the big picture. Even though the world is round and we can't see past the horizon, we *know* that there is more beyond. The same with wealth. We may not be able to see past our immediate financial horizon, but we have to believe our wealth is there.

My Million-Dollar Faith Story

Let me tell one last story to illustrate the power of believing.

It happened a few years ago, when I was just starting out as a speaker. I was hired by a pretty big company to come out to do a three-day seminar. "Robert, there's going to be at least three hundred people," my contacts promised. They also promised to pay me $500 per person. Well, I did the math and it looked pretty good—it added up to $150,000 for three days' work. So I signed the contract. Ordered more than three hundred books, workbooks, sets of CDs, and DVDs to have available. Shipped them. Bought an airline ticket for myself. And set out.

You can imagine my shock when I got there and only three people showed up! I'd spent several thousands of dollars on materials and travel.

The president was full of apologies. He offered to cancel the seminar. "Robert," he said, "I'll understand if you walk right out of here and never do business with our company again." On and on he went, apologizing, cussing, and then apologizing again.

But I said, "Look, three people traveled a long distance to get here, giving up their valuable time so they could take my seminar. Let's give them a great seminar."

All of us—me, the three participants, and the president—sat around a coffee table for three days, and I presented my seminar. Then I said good-bye to everyone. Packed up. And went back home.

Remember!
If you take two spiritual laws and add faith,
wealth will be your reward.

It wasn't until two years later that the Universe rewarded me. Out of the blue I got a call from one of the participants who'd attended that seminar. "Man," he said, "I'm sure you don't remember me, but I attended that seminar and I'd never seen anything like it. You were terrific. Even though I knew you were out a ton of dough and only three people showed up, you stayed and gave it your all. I never forgot that." Then he went on to tell me that he'd just launched a marketing company and wanted to show me what his firm could do for me on the Internet. Well, he showed me, all right. Within a year or so, he made me almost $500,000!

You never know when the universal laws of "getting" and "giving" are going to kick in. You just have to believe they will.

The Blog of Gold

I know I said just one more story, but this one is too good not to share. And again, it demonstrates the need for faith when dealing with the spiritual laws of wealth.

Most of the time I try to help or give to charities anonymously. But this one time I made a very private donation, which came back to bless me in a very public way. Let me tell you what happened.

During one of my seminars a man came up from the back of the room and said in front of everyone, "Robert, I really want to do well and get rich, but I've had a really hard time lately. The company I worked for went out of business, so I lost my job. I have no friends or family. Here I am, trying to build my life back, and today I couldn't make the rent and got thrown out of my apartment—so now I'm homeless. I never in my whole life thought this would happen to me. I don't want to embarrass myself, or you, Robert, but I'm desperate. I don't have any place to stay. I feel bad telling you this, but I need some advice. What can I do?"

He didn't ask for money. He asked for advice. And as a result, we both became richer that day.

"I can help you," I said. "I travel so much that I have all these reward points for hotel rooms. Instead of letting my points expire because I'll never be able to use them, I'm going to give them to you so you can have a room for a couple of days."

What I didn't tell him was that I had him upgraded to a suite—not just for a couple of days, but for ten days.

I never heard from him.

A few months later, as I went around the country speaking, the crowds at my seminars got bigger. I couldn't figure out why. I wasn't doing anything different. But then people in my seminars started to come up to me and say, "Robert, I signed up for your seminar because of this amazing letter I read on the Internet. And I'm going to buy all your stuff—and tell all my friends about you."

This happened over and over. Well, I'm on the road so much that I don't get to spend a lot of time online, so I couldn't figure out what letter they were talking about. Then one night I made a point to check it out for myself.

Sure enough, it was the guy I'd helped out with a hotel suite for ten days when he was homeless. He'd gone on every financial Web site and every blog and had written the story of how I'd helped him. His letter ended with the words "Robert is the real deal."

Those few reward points I gave to this man brought me hundreds of thousands of dollars of new business—a reward I hadn't imagined at all.

Balance

The main reason that I focus on the two spiritual laws of wealth—the law of getting and the law of giving—is for balance. There's a fulcrum in the Universe. On one side is the wealth that comes to you. You're the receiver of abundance. On the other side is the wealth that flows from you to others. You're the giver. Both of these are important. Both must be in perfect balance.

In fact, a friend of mine wears two silver bracelets. The one on her left wrist is to remind her to hold out her hand and receive. The one on her right wrist is to remind her to reach out her hand and give. Each is inscribed with one of the spiritual laws of wealth.

I've always thought that was a great way to keep the two laws never far from your thoughts. You can see those two bracelets on my Web site, www.GetRichWithRobert.com.

Let Go

Finally, just let go. Give yourself over to the energy of wealth. Trust in abundance and in your right to receive it and your generosity in sharing.

There's only one sure thing about the spiritual laws of wealth—they make all the difference in whether you become a Rich Idiot or remain a RUB.

Your Rich Idiot Upside-Down Action Plan
1. Write down five ways you're going to receive wealth.
2. Write down five ways you're going to give wealth.
3. Write down five things you're grateful for.
4. Write down three people you forgive.
5. Write down this statement and read it twice a day: *I receive the abundance of the Universe with thanks. I give generously to others.*

part **TWO**

A I M

secret no. 3

One Goal Makes You Rich, More Than One Keeps You Broke

All we seek is one goal, one goal.
All we need is one goal.
— EIFFEL 65

The Power of One

If you've been buying and reading tons of self-help books, you probably have long, long lists of goals. After all, that's what they all advocate. "You need goals," goes their mantra. And you need to write them down . . . you need to read them every single day . . . you need at least 101 of them—sound familiar?

A lot of these books also tell you to break down each of your mega-goals into subgoals. So now you've used up an entire ream of paper and have listed as a goal every single thing you hope to have, become, or accomplish. You've categorized and cataloged this unwieldy mass of goals into career, family, relationships, health, exercise and diet, leisure, income, savings, investments and wealth, and even spirit or soul goals.

You've listed the car you want, the house; the afternoons of Little League coaching you're going to do; the courses you're going to take; the tête-à-tête dinners you're going to schedule to keep the romance going; the vacations you're going to book; the proposal that's going to get you that promotion at work; the gym you're going to join; the weight you're going to lose; the water you're going to drink instead of vodka or beer; the weekly phone call you're going to make to your mom; the garage you're going to clean; the business you're going to start; the checkbook you're going to finally balance—whew!

How many of these goals have you actually achieved? How many *will* you achieve? What has this massive goal-writing exercise ever brought you except writer's cramp and an increasing sense of personal failure? Obviously your goal-setting mania hasn't yielded much—otherwise you wouldn't have bought this book, right? Goals and setting high goals is okay, but if it hasn't worked for you, maybe there's a better way.

Remember!
Setting too many goals is like taking aim with a shotgun.
Setting one goal is like taking aim with a laser beam.

Why *is* that? Well, it's kind of obvious when you stop and think about it. Writing down hundreds of goals scatters your focus and your energy. And that diffusion weakens your resolve and makes you vulnerable to feelings of failure. These feelings attract more failure. And eventually you give up. I know I'm right because before I became a Rich Idiot and learned how to set goals, I did the same thing—took aim at hundreds of targets and collected not a single bull's-eye.

So here's what I want you to do: Take all your goals and toss them in the garbage. That's right—in the garbage. (There, doesn't that feel liberating already?)

The truth is, Rich Idiots don't have lists and lists of goals. Rich Idiots have only *one* goal, but—and this is a very BIG but—they work toward that one goal every single day.

Remember!
Rich Idiots have only one goal.
Rich Idiots work toward that goal every day.

Here's the Only Goal You Need

So what's the goal? The goal is to become a Rich Idiot—duh! Because once you become a Rich Idiot you'll be living your perfect life. You'll have the two things that Rich Idiots have: money and time.

You'll have the money for that dream home, that luxury car, those vacations; you'll have the means to look after your family and the resources to contribute to your community and the world. Like me, you'll be able to do all those things and never work another day in your life. That's the money part of reaching your goal.

You'll also have the time to look after the needs of your body and soul, and you'll have the time to help others. I've been blessed with enough wealth to be able to help support two special schools for kids who were thrown out of regular schools (kind of like me), as well as an international charity that feeds and houses over a thousand orphans and street kids—the discarded children of drug addicts. Also, I'm able to give away a house to a single mom and her children almost every year. But that's not all. I'm able to read and study and contemplate. I have the time to learn and think.

Repeat after me: *What's my goal? To become a Rich Idiot!* There, you've just set your goal. How hard was that?

Remember!
The most important goal is this: What activity am I
going to do today? The Rich Idiot takes action.

Three Things to Goal Success

Now that you've set your goal, you've got to do three things to reach
it. That's right, only three things.

Here's the first:

1. Decide how much money will make you a Rich Idiot.

Here's the second:

2. Choose the path you're going to take to reach your Rich Idiot
   goal.

Here's the third:

3. Pick activities to do every day to take you to your goal.

I've made these three things really easy. They're only going to take
you a few minutes.

Step No. 1: Write Yourself a Rich Idiot Wealth Check

I remember watching an episode of *Oprah* with actor Jim Carrey, who
shared an amazing story. He told how he was broke and practically living in his car, and then one day he wrote himself a check for ten million dollars for acting, dated it for Thanksgiving a year down the road,

and tucked it into his wallet. I was riveted, as was the entire audience, when he said that an offer came in for him to do the movie *Dumb and Dumber.* The offer came in on Thanksgiving Day exactly one year later!

Pretty powerful stuff. And if it worked for Jim Carrey, it can work for you. Here's a wealth check all ready to go. Just fill one out. Don't leave any blanks. I have copies on my Web site, www.GetRichWith Robert.com.

- Put in the date by which you want to become a Rich Idiot. The date is important because it forces you to commit to a time horizon. Without a date, the check is meaningless—more a vague wish than part of your powerful goal.
- Put in the exact amount that you believe will make you a Rich Idiot. As Donald Trump says, "If you're going to dream—dream big." Remember, this dollar amount is for your entire Rich Idiot dream. It must be enough to buy you all the toys you want, provide for your family, give you the lifestyle you crave, and make it possible for you to help others. This is the first place to be generous. Be generous to yourself.
- Put in the services you'll render to earn your Rich Idiot pay. This is important. It's not enough to say, "I'm going to be a Rich Idiot," and sit back and expect the Universe to make you one. You have to be prepared to do something, to give something for the money and the life of a Rich Idiot. Jim Carrey wrote that he'd provide "acting services" in exchange for his wealth. What services will *you* provide? If you're not sure, don't worry. By the time you've finished this book, you'll be able to fill out that service line with enthusiasm, passion, and confidence.
- Sign your wealth check and put it into your wallet. Your signature is your bond. It's what makes this check a contract. It's your pledge that you'll make good on this check. By keeping it in your wallet where you can see it every time you put in or take out money, you'll reinforce its power.

at's it. That's Step No. 1.

ou're done. How easy was that?

Remember, the faster you fill out the check, the faster you'll start becoming a Rich Idiot.

My Wealth Check   Date_____

Pay to the

Order of _____ **$**_____

                          Your Name

For _____ _____

          Services Rendered   **Your Signature**

Warning!

Be very careful who you share your goal with.
Most people will criticize it; few will support it.
Want some goal encouragement? I'll support your goal
and help you get there. Just visit me on my
Web site, www.GetRichWithRobert.com.

Step No. 2: Write Yourself a Rich Idiot Mission Statement

What's a mission statement? It's a few sentences that sum up what you want your life to be. But it's the most important piece of personal writing you can do. One of the best examples of the power of a personal mission statement surfaces in the 1996 movie *Jerry Maguire*. When the movie opens, Jerry is struggling, trying to figure out his life—what he stands for, what's important to him. So he writes a long personal statement. (Don't panic: His was too long; yours only needs to be a few words.) It's that mission statement that propels Jerry to act the way he acts—to go out on his own, test his value system, win the woman he loves, and ultimately build a life that fulfills him.

Anyone and everyone who has ever been super successful has a clear mission statement. Before you write your own mission statement, remember, it's all about you. It's your opportunity to think about what you really want, what you're good at, what ignites your passion, how you want to live the rest of your life. Ready? Let's get started.

My Rich Idiot Mission Statement

This is so easy. All you have to do is fill in the blanks. So go get a pen or pencil.

1. My Values Sentence

I want to be known and remembered for _____
_____.

This is all about you and what's important to you. You have only the one life, as we all do. Here's where you decide how you're going to spend it. This is the sentence in which you write down your values. My own values sentence went something like this:

"I want to be known and remembered for <u>having devoted myself to my family, being a good human being, creating great wealth, and using that wealth to help others</u>."

2. My Passion Sentence

I'm really good at and passionate about _____
_____,

and this will become my key to unlocking the Rich Idiot vault.

A very wise man once said, "Have fun doing whatever it is you desire to accomplish . . . and do it because you love it, not because it's work." I completely agree. This is about what you'd do if you had all the money in the world. Rich Idiots know that first comes the passion—then the money! My own passion sentence said:

"I'm really good at and passionate about <u>helping others find homes and making an ethical profit through that pursuit</u>, and this will become my key to unlocking the Rich Idiot vault." And that's exactly what happened.

3. My Action Sentence

I commit myself to _____

every day in pursuit of my one goal.

This is key. Without action, even your one goal cannot be achieved. Remember, it's not the goal that's the problem for most RUBs—rather, it's the daily doing of simple tasks to reach that goal. All you need is the one goal. BUT you've got to work toward that goal, act on that goal, every single day. My own action sentence read something like this: *"I commit myself to <u>doing at least three things</u> every day in pursuit of my one goal."*

Step No. 3: Pick Activities to Do Every Day

The last and most important step to setting your goal is to activate it. Rich Idiots do *something* every single day to get closer to their goal. What are you going to do today? What are you going to do tomorrow? The next day? And the next? Commit yourself to an activity or two or three and write them down.

Today I'm going to _____.

Tomorrow I'm going to _____.

The next day I'm going to _____.

And so on.

That's it. Rich Idiot goal setting in a nutshell. And because it's so simple and you've already done it, there is no action plan at the end of this chapter. Go ahead: Pat yourself on the back. Relax. And get ready to learn exactly how to reach your goal quickly.

secret no. 4

To Be Rich Tomorrow, You Must Live Rich Today

In the moment you ask, and believe *and* know *you already have it in the unseen, the entire Universe shifts to bring it into the seen. You must act, speak, and think, as though you are receiving it* now. *Why? The Universe is a mirror, and the law of attraction is mirroring back to you your dominant thoughts. So doesn't it make sense that you have to see yourself as receiving it? If your thoughts contain noticing you do not have it yet, you will continue to attract not having it yet. You must believe you have it already. You must believe you have received it. You have to emit the feeling frequency of having received it, to bring those pictures back as your life. When you do that, the law of attraction will powerfully move all circumstances, people, and events, for you to receive. . . . How do you get yourself to a point of believing? Start make-believing. Be like a child, and make-believe. Act as if you have it already. As you make-believe, you will begin to believe you have received. . . . Have faith. Your belief that you have it, that undying faith, is your greatest power. When you believe you are receiving, get ready, and watch the magic begin!*

— RHONDA BYRNE, *THE SECRET*

Why Are You in an UnRich Rut?

If you're like most RUBs (Remember—Right side Up and Broke?) you live according to very strict conditions. You think these conditions will bring you wealth in some hazy and distant future. You impose limitations on your present lifestyle and the pleasure you could be deriving from it.

Here's what you tell yourself: I'll have all the things I want when I get rich. I'll live the life I'm dreaming about when I get rich. I'll have all the time I need when I get rich. I'll enjoy my family and friends when I get rich. Guess what? That's absolutely the wrong way to set about getting rich. Actually, it's the "right side up" way, which, in the world of Rich Idiots, as you know by now, is the wrong way. If you start by postponing all the goodies and treats that would make you feel like a success you'll never become a success. Why? Because you believe—quite wrongly—that your wealth will come in the future. Rich Idiots know that their wealth is right now, in the present, and they live accordingly.

Don't Play the Waiting Game

Rich Idiots know that to get rich tomorrow, you must live rich today. So many "wannabe wealthies" miss that point. Let me share my story with you. I was brought up like most people—to get a job, work until you're sixty-five, have fun for a few years, and then you die.

Well, that didn't make any sense to me. I wanted to live well *now*. I didn't want to wait until I was sixty or seventy to travel or live wherever I wanted. I didn't want to spend my entire life working and dreaming of my wealthy future. I wanted to live my perfect life now and enjoy it for years and years. I was all about living rich in the present, not saving it all up for a future that might never materialize.

What did living well right now mean? It meant enjoying all the toys of the wealthy—the clothes, the cars, the travel, the luxury, the goodies. That was the material Rich Idiot in me. But as you already know, I also believe that to be a Rich Idiot you also have to have time—a precious gift you share with others. Rich Idiots spend real time with their families. They give to their communities. They give to charities, support their religious and educational institutions. They're benefactors of the arts and sciences. They help others climb out of poverty and reach their own peak. I wanted to become a spiritual Rich Idiot as well. I wanted it all. I wanted a full, happy, successful life! And I wanted it *now*.

Imagine my surprise when I discovered I wasn't the only Rich Idiot who thought that way. Rich Idiots live in the moment—in every single moment. Rich Idiots live the life they dream about, except they live it every day while they're wide awake.

Remember!
Rich Idiots don't wait for wealth they *don't* have—
they live the wealth they *do* have.

That's one of the most important secrets you'll learn.

RUBs live in the future and ignore the riches of the present. If you keep telling yourself you can't have or can't afford the life you want today, you'll send out a signal that says just that. And the result will be predictable—you won't ever be able to afford your dream life. Your attitude will keep you from feeling wealthy and attracting wealth. When you tell yourself you have to wait, that message acts to repel wealth and hold it at bay. Contrast that with the "I have it all now" message. The result? The wealth magnet will draw abundance to you. See the difference? Stop saying you have to wait for wealth. And start living the wealth you have right now. And believe me, you have more wealth right now than you ever imagined. I'm going to help you uncover it and use it. Too many people live a life of what I call "contingent happiness and success." That is, when something happens in the future, then they allow themselves to be happy. Don't wait. Be it now. Why not?

The Past, the Present, the Future

You're reading this book because you want to change your life. You want to go from your past, which may represent scarcity, to a future you hope will be filled with abundance. That's great. But don't forget to make a stop in the present.

Let's take a look at a typical RUB. Maybe this is you. You look at the past and you hate it. There were days or months or even years when you were broke, when creditors were hounding you, when you didn't know where the money to pay your bills would come from. The past wasn't a feel-good place for you. So you picked up this book hoping to find a better future. You want the rich life you know you deserve. You want the status symbols, the security, and the success you know wealth can bring. And this book will deliver that future to you. But this book is also going to give you a huge bonus right now—you don't have to wait for your wealth ship to come in—because I'm going to show you how to live rich right now and why you have to.

The Present Is Where the Real Wealth Is

Think about it. Think about where you are right now. You're in the present. But if you're like most RUBs, you're still thinking about your broke past with one half of your brain, and wishing for future wealth with the other. Stop that right now. Get out of the past. If you focus on your past problems you'll block your future wealth.

Here's how Rich Idiots handle that critical gap between the past they want to leave and the future they hope to have. They "fake it" in the present. That's right. The best way to lose the past and accelerate the future is to pretend the future has arrived. And this upside-down way of thinking is one of the major Rich Idiot secrets.

Remember!
Rich Idiots fake it until they make it.

The Science Behind "Fake It Till You Make It"

This concept is very powerful and very real. One of the greatest scientists of our time has attested to it. Albert Einstein said, "When I examine myself and my methods of thought, I come to the conclusion that the gift of fantasy has meant more to me than my talent for absorbing positive knowledge."

Prevention magazine reports, "Studies looking at the 'fake it till you make it' approach show that it can have a surprisingly strong and immediate impact on your emotions."

Other researchers call this strategy a shortcut to success. Will Edwards, the founder of White Dove Books, wrote about it this way:

> If you would like to achieve success really quickly—in any field of endeavor—you might consider taking a little shortcut which is known as NLP (Neuro-Linguistic Programming) "modeling." To make use of this technique, what you need to do is to first think of someone you know who is already achieving the success you're after. Just try to do that now . . . see if you can think of someone who fits the bill; someone who is already successful doing the very activity you need to improve. Once you have identified your "model" you need to analyze exactly what it is that person is actually doing to produce the results. Once you know what your model is actually doing, you can work on doing the same things and, by the law of cause and effect, you can also produce the same results. The modeling approach is

sometimes referred to as "fake it till you make it" but there is nothing fake about it. You're simply using a scientific approach to the analysis of methods. . . . Eventually, those new behaviors—the ones that are producing the results—will sink deep into your own personality and you'll change for the better. So ultimately, you'll not need to "fake it" because you'll become the genuine article.

The Sweet Payoff

This "fake it till you make it" or "act as if" strategy has been used by some of the most successful people of our time.

Earl Nightingale tells how even when he was a lowly announcer at a smallish radio station in Phoenix he dreamed of becoming a network announcer. To fuel his dream, every time he was on the radio he pretended that he was standing at the microphone in a major network studio and that his voice was going out over the airwaves to millions of people. Every spare minute he had, he listened to the network announcers whose ranks he wanted to join. Pretty soon he sounded just like someone with an audience in the millions.

What was he doing? He was pretending he'd hit the big time. He was performing the role of a national radio personality. He was "faking it until he made it."

What happened next was even more interesting.

After serving his "apprenticeship" for eighteen months or so in Phoenix, Earl took himself to Chicago—home of the big boys. Armed with his dream and his year and a half of practicing his vision every minute, he secured a couple of interviews with two of the top radio stations in the market. As he tells it,

I'll never forget that first day in those beautiful, posh surroundings—the marble floors, the uniformed elevator starters, those fabulous brass and glistening hardwood elevators. . . . The studio was as impressive as the rest of the place, very large for one thing, with a concert grand piano and sound-effects paraphernalia. I walked to the standing microphone and looked into the darkened engineer's room beyond the slanting glass. I began . . .

Can you guess how this story ends? What do you think all that "faking" did for Earl? Let's find out what happened. Let's let Earl finish his story.

I not only had the job, I was under contract for more money than I had dreamed of earning.

Yeah, But . . .

A lot of people say to me, "Yeah, but I can't live in the present, Robert. I can't 'fake it till I make it.'" Then they proceed to give me this whole list of reasons why:

- I can't afford it.
- I don't have the time.
- It's not how I was brought up.
- People will think I'm a snob.
- That's not really me—I'm a blue jeans kind of person.

The Importance of Rich Idiot Role-Playing

So what do I tell this *yeah, but* crowd? Listen up.

I say, if you tell yourself you can't afford it, you're teaching yourself to think "broke" instead of "rich." That's not going to make you a Rich Idiot. What you should be asking is "How *can* I afford it?" or

"How *can* I get the same wealthy feeling with the resources I have?" Rich Idiots think, "How can I," not "I can't."

You tell me you don't have time. I say, everyone has exactly the same amount of time: twenty-four hours a day, 365 days a year. You need to start spending time doing what will make you a Rich Idiot. Rich Idiots work for time more than they work for money.

You tell me it's not how you were brought up. I say, we were all raised hearing the same stuff: "Don't go outside without a coat, you'll catch cold." In reality, going outside without a coat isn't the cause of colds; viruses are. It's just one in a long list of "lies" we're told in order to keep us obeying rules. If you still believe those lies and still follow rules, you're going to remain a RUB. Instead, question everything and decide on the validity of each statement you hear. Every time you hear "You're not smart enough" or "You're not good enough" or "You'll never make it," ask yourself, "Is this true or is this just another one of those lies like the one about catching a cold without a coat?" Then change each of those statements to "I *am* smart enough" and "I *am* good enough" and "I *will* make it!" And just watch your successful re-sults. Rich Idiots think for themselves.

You tell me people will think you're a snob. I say, start hanging around with different people. A good friend would want you to be suc-cessful, wealthy, and living your perfect life. If that's not what you're hearing from your friends and family, tune them out and move on.

You tell me you wouldn't feel comfortable. I know what you mean. Where does that come from? Right now, today, you have got to deal with this issue and be comfortable with yourself, as a happy, wealthy, successful person.

Get Rid of Your "Stinking Thinking"

Get rid of that "stinking thinking," because you *do* deserve the best. You *can* have the best. You *are* the best. Replace any other self-deprecating, negative thoughts with these Rich Idiot thoughts.

Think about what's best for you. What is your perfect life like? What do you want to accomplish? What do you want to contribute? What do you want to enjoy today and leave behind for tomorrow? Answer that and you're ready to become a Rich Idiot right now!

Okay, Robert, So How *Do* I Live Rich Today When I'm Broke Today?

"How do I live rich today when I'm really broke today?" you ask. I'm going to give you lots of ways to do just that. But first I want to share a story my friend Kaye told me about what happened to her the day she discovered this particular Rich Idiot secret—that is, to be rich tomorrow, you must live rich today.

> It was November, over twenty years ago, and I was in New York City. I was looking for a job. I had two small babies to look after, and the little money I had was quickly running out.
>
> Day after drizzling day I walked up and down those cold sidewalks with no luck. By late afternoon of the fourth day, I realized I had just enough money for another two days—if I was very careful.
>
> It was getting dark, and a damp wind rushed through the trees of Central Park and chilled me to the bone. I thought of a bowl of hot soup and turned a corner, looking for a coffee shop. Instead, I found myself in front of the magnificent Plaza Hotel.
>
> Something, maybe just the longing for warmth, pulled me inside. The lobby blazed with lights. A Strauss waltz filled the air, competing gently with the sound of laughter and the clink of porcelain cups against fine china saucers. Afternoon tea was being served at the Plaza's famous Palm Court lobby restaurant.

The maître d' approached me, and without thinking I asked for a table for one. He seated me and handed me the menu. I glanced at the prices. Tea at the Plaza would cost me almost the rest of my precious meal money.

But my feet hurt and it felt good to sit down. Perched on my gilded chair at the tiny table covered by a heavy linen cloth, I felt rich. I liked the feeling. I'd been feeling broke and scared and alone for so long that it felt good to pretend I was one of the wealthy ones—to pretend I belonged.

And because I'm a talker, because I was lonely, because I wanted so very badly to belong, and connect with another human being in that cold city, I started to chatter away to the waiting maître d'. I blurted out how I was looking for work. That I had two babies at home I needed to support. That this tea was costing me the rest of my precious meal money and that a bowl of soup in a coffee shop or a burger would have been much more sensible. I told him that I had just wanted to feel special for a few minutes in this enchanted room where all the lights sparkled, all the people were beautiful, and the music filled my soul.

That maître d' didn't say a word. So finally I ordered a pot of tea. He just listened, then turned away, looking pretty stern. I felt stupid for opening my heart and my mouth to a complete stranger.

But I eased off my shoes and pressed my aching toes into the warm, soft carpet. The music soared over me. For that moment I felt safe. I felt as though I belonged. I closed my eyes.

When I opened them again, the maître d' was standing in front of me. Instead of the tea I was expecting, in one hand he held a bottle of French champagne and in the other a huge bowl of winter strawberries. He placed both on the table in front of me, smiled, and said, "Welcome to New

York, compliments of the Plaza." I looked at him and my eyes filled with tears of gratitude. In that instant I knew I was rich . . . and going to be richer.

The very next day I found a job. I made a home. I raised my two babies. And every year I went back to the Plaza for tea. The lights would blaze. The music would soar. And I'd slip out of my shoes and press my feet into the warm, soft carpet. And every year that same kind man who'd brought me the wealth of friendship on that lonely day served me French champagne and strawberries.

And then he died. Now every year in November I go back to the Plaza and imagine we're together. I bring a basket and we share a bowl of winter strawberries and a glass of French champagne. He became my friend and I was not alone. And I credit my success and my wealth today to that one afternoon when I pretended I was wealthy in New York.

Why do you think I told you Kaye's story? She had a choice. She could choose to be a RUB or a Rich Idiot.

She could have sat in a garishly lit coffee shop, on a red vinyl bench. She could have picked up a stained menu and ordered a cheap burger and greasy fries. She could have drunk her coffee from a thick pottery mug. She could have ripped open a tiny pot of fake cream and a paper packet of sugar and stirred the whole thing with a bent spoon. That would have been the sensible thing to do, given that she was broke. But that would have made her a RUB.

Remember!
Rich Idiots believe they deserve the best
that life has to offer.

Kaye knew deep down inside that she wasn't a RUB but rather was a Rich Idiot. She knew instinctively it was better to sit under a crystal chandelier on an embroidered chair. She knew it was better to enjoy winter strawberries served on a china plate. She knew the strains of a Strauss waltz were more soothing for her soul than the jarring grind of city traffic. She knew she deserved the finer things in life. She wasn't a Rich Idiot yet, but she knew she'd never become one unless she "faked it till she made it." What about you?

Create a Wealth Wall

It's important that you get very comfortable with looking, feeling, and acting like a Rich Idiot. One of the best ways to do that and to attract all the wonderful pleasures of wealth is to create a wealth wall. Think of it as a prop, as a necessary tool on your way to your new life. (See a sample at www.GetRichWithRobert.com.)

Find an empty wall—it could be in your bedroom, your bathroom, or even your closet, as long as it's a place that you see twice a day, once in the morning and once before you go to bed. Now go out and buy yourself a large picture frame—the kind that holds awards and diplomas—and hang that empty frame on the wall.

Next cut out pictures and words of everything you would have and do if you had unlimited wealth and were living your perfect life right now. Clip photos of cars, houses, vacations, tropical islands, clothes, and jewelry. Go ahead and cut out lots of dollar signs. Don't forget the yacht, the private jet, and those mansions. Indulge yourself. Add awards, degrees, and other symbols of recognition you crave. Also cut out photos of the famous people you'd like to meet. Cut out front covers of all the magazines you want to be featured in, the headlines you want to make.

Now that your wealth wall is loaded with toys, go back and get serious. Add the real wealth. Add the dreams that really stir your soul. Cut out images of the life you want for your family—the schools for your children, the comforts of security for your spouse, your parents, and your siblings. Find pictures of how you'd all spend precious moments together if you gave those you love the gift of time.

You're not done yet. To be a true Rich Idiot you've got to get past the playpen stage, with all its toys, and even the personal "people I love" stage and really begin to create wealth that can be shared with the world. As Andrew Carnegie, one of America's greatest Rich Idiots and philanthropists, said, "I resolved to stop accumulating and begin the infinitely more serious and difficult task of wise distribution." Plan to do what Carnegie did. Find depictions of good works. Add scholarships you could sponsor. Kids you could send to camp. Single parents you could help. Villages you could feed. Medicines you could ship. Schools you could build and staff. Go ahead and stretch your wealth.

You're almost done building your wealth wall. Just one more thing to add: a big smiling picture of yourself!

This wealth wall is one of the most powerful tools of wealth—a full-color daily inspiration that will lead you to achievements beyond your wildest dreams.

You can also use wealth magnets to keep your wealth vision focused. Find these at www.GetRichWithRobert.com.

Robert's Personal Secrets for Living Rich Today

Let me share some of the secrets Rich Idiots everywhere use to live the way they do. Let me show you how many Rich Idiots *really* afford the designer clothes, luxury cars, first-class travel and vacations, unbelievable homes, and the best dinners in the finest restaurants. How they manage to save *and* give at the same time. Simply put, they keep their wealth chart.

What am I talking about? Here's a formula that will open your eyes to how much (as a percentage of their after-tax income) Rich Idiots spend compared with RUBs. Please take note of how these numbers compare to your own lifestyle and spending patterns. Remember, numbers don't lie.

Category	RUBs	Rich Idiots
Housing	40%	30%
Transportation	30%	10%
Insurance/medical	10%	10%
Food and clothing	20%	15%
Travel/entertainment	20%	15%
Savings	0%	10%
Charity	0%	10%
Total	**120%**	**100%**

Check out what this means. It shows that some RUBs are in debt up to the tune of 20 percent a year *and* they haven't given a penny to charity or put any dimes into their own savings account. Rich Idiots, on the other hand, have saved 10 percent of their income every year, they're debt-free, and they're able to give money to others so that more comes back to them. What does *your* wealth chart look like—like that of a RUB or a Rich Idiot?

If you want to be rich tomorrow, start living rich today.

Double Your Money

First you have to double your money—your income—fast. You're going to need more money to turn your RUB wealth chart into a Rich Idiot wealth chart. You're going to need more money to save, to give away to charities, to be able to afford the "fake it till you make it" lifestyle of Rich Idiots.

Don't panic. I hear you saying, "Robert, I'm already working two jobs and I'm still barely keeping my head above the rising level of bills and interest rates." I'm not saying that to double your income you should take on a third job. In fact, by the time you finish reading this book, you'll have the knowledge and the tools and the confidence to stop working for others altogether and start working for yourself and those you love. Please understand that when I say you have to double your income, it doesn't imply working harder. On the contrary, it means working less but bringing in more. Working for added value. It means getting more for what you spend. It means being able to afford the lifestyle of a Rich Idiot without paying RUB prices.

It's About Value—Not Money

First, Rich Idiots almost never pay retail prices for anything. Rich Idiots always increase their spendable income by reducing the cost of the material things they want to buy. Rich Idiots understand one of Robert's Rules: Everything has two prices. One is the "open to the public" retail price—the one that's on the listing for your dream house. It's the sticker price of that car you really want. It's the price on the cute outfit in the boutique, the price of that beautiful pair of earrings in the jeweler's window, the price the travel agent quotes when you go to purchase your ticket or vacation package.

But that's not the Rich Idiot price. Rich Idiots pay a different price—sometimes as much as 25 or 75 percent less than retail. Rich Idiots shop wholesale.

How can you get the wholesale price, too? It's easy. Which brings me to my second way to become wealthy. Always negotiate for a better price, a lower price, a better deal, more benefits.

Remember!
Rich Idiots always ask for more *and* for less—
more value and less cost.

The following story illustrates what I mean. I was traveling with two Rich Idiot friends of mine (well, one was a Mega-Rich Idiot). When we got to our hotel we were told that no $200 rooms were available but several suites were—at a price of $1,500 each. Two of us had started to take out our credit cards when our mega-rich friend stopped us. "Go and get a cup of coffee," he suggested, "and let me take care of checking us in." We did. Half an hour later we came back and he handed each of us a key to a suite. "This is too much," we protested, thinking he'd paid for our accommodations. "You're darn right," he replied. "Their price was too much, so I bargained them down to $99 per suite! Robert," he added, "you never 'get' if you don't ask."

At first I felt uncomfortable knowing that this immensely wealthy man, who could have easily afforded a dozen suites at the $1,500 price point, had spent half an hour negotiating the price down to the "ouch" level. And then it occurred to me: He really *is* a Rich Idiot. He got a fantastic suite and paid less for it than he would have for a motel room. He was happy. The hotel was happy because it had filled what would otherwise have been empty suites. And that amazing Mega-Rich Idiot had just added $1,400 to his net worth—money he could now invest to produce even more riches. How had he managed to accomplish this? He asked for a discount and kept on asking until he got the best possible deal.

Warning!
Nothing works all the time. But if you *never* ask,
it will *never* work. Guaranteed.

Rich Idiot Shopping Spree

When it comes to shopping, what, specifically, do Rich Idiots do? They find the real bargains. It doesn't matter where you live; it doesn't matter how much money you have right now. You want to find those Rich Idiot shopping secrets that I discovered on my own road to wealth (ones I still use every day). Let's start by going on a typical Rich Idiot shopping spree for your dream house, your dream car, your dream vacation, your dream wardrobe, and a seat in your dream restaurant. And then I'm going to show you how to start your dream savings plan and make your first contribution to a charity. Ready?

Remember!
A Rich Idiot shopping spree is less money spent—
and more value bought.

---

1. Housing
Yes, You *Can* Have Your Dream House Today

Let's start with housing, because that's the single biggest expense for almost everyone. You've got a house or an apartment. You hate the neighborhood. You hate the house. You hate the landlord. You hate your neighbors. All you can think of is how much you don't want to live there. The solution is simple: Move. It's even simpler than that: Move into your dream home right now.

Before you start giving me all the *yeah*, *buts* again, here are more ways that Rich Idiots afford to live rich—and, yes, that includes me.

Number 1: Negotiate Your Rent or Mortgage

If you've been a good tenant, the landlord will want to hold on to you and will often pay or upgrade you to a better apartment just to make sure you don't move out. If you own your own home and have a mortgage, shop around for the best deal in refinancing. You can negotiate every aspect of this—the closing cost, the points, the term, the interest rate; everything is negotiable. And every dollar you save is a dollar you can invest in becoming richer.

I want to add a word here about negotiating. Negotiating is just asking. It's not "beating someone up"; it's not taking unfair advantage of the other person; it's not creating a win-or-lose scenario. Negotiating is creating a win-win outcome where both people walk

away satisfied with the results. There is one magic question good ne-
gotiators always ask: "Can you do any better?"

Number 2: Share Your Space

Go get the bigger place of your dreams and rent out some of the
bedrooms to others. Share your space. I did this myself and found an
amazing house in the best part of town with four huge bedrooms. I
took the lease on the property and linked up with three suitable and
eager roommates. Don't think roommates are just for your college
years or early in your career. You can rent to exchange students, executives on assignment, visiting professors—there are many appealing
possibilities.

I have a friend who needed to work in New York for six months.
She didn't want to commit to a long lease. She went to a roommate-
matching service and found a widow with a huge apartment on Fifth
Avenue. My friend became her roommate and lived in one of New
York's most luxurious buildings, with a view of Central Park and a
daily maid, a doorman, and the cachet of a Fifth Avenue address, all for
much less than she would have paid for a tiny apartment on her own.
And there was a bonus, too: She made a wonderful new friend.

Number 3: House-sit

Some of my Rich Idiot friends house-sit for other Rich Idiots who
are away on holidays or spending the season in one of their other
homes. Both parties enjoy a win-win situation. If you're the "beginning Rich Idiot," you get to live in some of the most magnificent
houses, with all the trappings of wealth, just for "babysitting" the
property. And believe me, nothing makes you feel more rich than living rich.

Number 4: Get a Lease Option

Leasing with an option to buy is a popular way to live rich. It
comes with many benefits and few negatives. In fact, I'm currently

using a lease-purchase agreement to live in one of the best buildings on South Beach.

Here's what you do:

- Find the location you want.
- In that area, look for properties that are For Sale by Owner. Note especially those that have been on the market for a while. Then offer to lease the property from the owner with an option to purchase it in the future at a predetermined price.

How does doing that make you a Rich Idiot? Well, let's say you find a property worth $600,000. If you owned it you'd be paying about $3,500 to $4,000 in mortgage, interest, insurance, and taxes. But if you lease-option it, your rent will likely be about $1,500 to $2,000 a month. Now you're living in an amazing place for a lot less than you would if you owned it. A part of your rent goes toward purchasing it— if you decide you want to buy it. You have the benefits of watching your lease-option property appreciate, and your credit isn't affected. If you want to start living rich right now, this is a totally fantastic idea.

Number 5: Follow the Thirty-Minute Rule

You'll find that by looking for a home just thirty minutes farther away from the center of town in any direction, you'll be able to afford almost twice the house for half the cost. I have friends who moved to Washington, D.C. They found that just a basic cramped three-bedroom home in the center of D.C. would cost them over $1 million. Imagine their shock—and delight—when they discovered that for every fifteen minutes they traveled away from the center of D.C., the houses got correspondingly bigger and cheaper. They settled on a beautiful five-bedroom home with a three-car garage sitting on an acre of land in a small community, forty-five minutes from town. The price? Just $220,000.

That's not the end of these Rich Idiots' success stories. Let me tell you about the huge bonus that accrued to them. It wasn't long before other home buyers discovered the same secret and began to purchase properties in the same small town, which drove prices up. Naturally, my friends' home appreciated. Just one year after they made the purchase the house was worth $310,000! Not bad. These people were living the rich life *and* making tons of money fast, too. They simply turned their thinking upside down—from city to country!

2. Transportation
Yes, You *Can* Have Your Dream Car Today

Now that you're living in your new home, let's get you a car to go with it. We all recognize that a car is more than transportation—it's a status symbol. Rich Idiots know that, too, but they get the status without the hefty price tag. Here's how.

Number 1: Buy Used Cars, Not New Ones

Rich Idiots who own luxury cars never buy them new, they always buy them used. And that includes me. I've owned a Jaguar, a Mercedes, and an Infinity—and every single one of them I bought after some RUB had purchased it new, driven it out of the showroom, and immediately lost 30 percent or more of its value.

How do I do it? I read the paper looking for car bargains, and when I find one, I snap it up. Several years ago I bought what was back then a $40,000 Jaguar for $18,000. That was less than most RUBs were paying for just an average car. Right now I'm driving an $85,000 Mercedes that I paid $44,000 for. How did I get such great deals? I teamed up with a car wholesaler. He went to a car auction on my behalf and found me the car. I paid him his nominal fee. And now I'm driving around in a car that originally cost a small fortune for about the same price a brand-new everyday vehicle costs. I'll drive that car for a year or so and I guarantee you that when I sell it I'll get back practically the entire amount I paid for it. So I drive a great car almost for free. That's what makes me a Rich Idiot.

Let me tell you a story about a friend of mine who loves everything British—including Rolls-Royce automobiles. Every two years he buys a classic Rolls for around $50,000. He drives this ultimate status symbol of wealth and success. And because these cars are no longer being made, every year they become more rare and more expensive. And here's the ultimate Rich Idiot success story: He often sells the Rolls back to the dealership for *more* than he paid for it. The dealer basically *pays him* for owning and driving a luxury automobile. You can do the same thing.

Number 2: Stop Owning and Start Leasing

There are times to own things and there are times to lease them. A car is one of those things that sometimes makes better money sense to lease rather than to own. Why? All your money isn't tied up in a depreciating asset, and a lease payment is often less than a loan payment, freeing up even more cash for other investments.

3. Insurance and Medical
Yes, You *Can* Protect Yourself and Your Family

Rich Idiots know that to ensure good health and protect assets, quality insurance is crucial. But let's face it: There isn't a lot of wiggle room available in this category. So here's my personal strategy: Get with a professional to determine the best monthly payments and the biggest deductible you can comfortably afford. That's it. It's simple. Keep as much money as you can right now; later in this book, you'll learn how to make it work for you to build your wealth.

4. Food and Clothing
Yes, You *Can* Dine in Your Dream Restaurant Today

One of the very best benefits of living like a Rich Idiot is that you'll begin to eat like one and probably get thinner and healthier in the process. Why do I say that? Because Rich Idiots don't eat in fast-food restaurants; they eat in upscale places where the portions are more controlled, the ingredients are fresher, and the atmosphere reflects wealth, not calories. Rich Idiots shop for healthy foods in ways that guarantee the best in freshness and in price.

Number 1: Go to the Best Restaurant in Town

If you want to hang out where the Rich Idiots do, then find the best restaurant or bistro in town and go there. Even if you can afford only a glass of iced tea and a salad, your body and your mind and your self-esteem will be better off. And remember to tip well. You'll be remembered and welcomed back when you return.

Number 2: Shop Smart

Shop smart. Join a price club like Costco or Sam's Club to save on food. Or visit your local farmers' market to buy direct from growers. Their food is fresher and more wholesome than much of the prepackaged stuff found in grocery stores.

Yes, You *Can* Wear Your Dream Wardrobe Today

When I was starting out I was one of the best-dressed real-estate entrepreneurs in Nashville, even though I didn't have the money for fancy clothes; I shopped at the local consignment stores. There I paid $80 for $1,000 suits that had hardly been worn. I wore a magnificent watch that cost me less than one I could purchase in a department store. And that's when I really learned the value of looking rich as a prerequisite to getting rich. I found when I dressed in my "success" suit of clothes, bankers believed in me, lawyers treated me with respect, and mortgage brokers offered me better deals, because I looked like a successful real-estate entrepreneur. *Looking* the part went a long way to *becoming* what I was dressed up to be.

Number 1: Shop in Consignment, Discount, and Outlet Stores

Today, I don't frequent consignment shops, but I do shop in discount stores and outlet malls. I love Syms and Filene's Basement, and I never stop looking for real bargains in clothing, shoes, jewelry, and accessories.

Number 2: Ask if a Sale Is Coming Up

If I'm in a regular department store or boutique, I ask the salesclerk if the item I'm contemplating purchasing will be on sale soon. You can't believe the number of times I've been told, "Yes, we're putting it on sale next week, but because you're here now, we would be pleased to offer you the sale price." Even in department stores I sometimes pay anywhere from 10 to 50 percent less than the person in front of me in line did for the exact same item.

5. Travel and Entertainment
Yes, You *Can* Have Your Dream Vacation Today

I love to travel. I love to travel first-class. I love to stay in the best hotels and resorts. But like most Rich Idiots, I hate to pay full price for this lifestyle. So what did I learn to do? I noticed that travel agents get discounts—often big discounts—for booking travel. They also get lots of perks, like upgrades from coach to business class or first class on a plane or from a simple room with no view to a huge ocean-front suite. Often travel agents are even offered free trips to fantastic destinations. So what does a Rich Idiot do?

Number 1: Become a Travel Agent

I decided to sign up to be a travel agent. It was as easy as filling out a form and joining an organization. Now I get major discounts and commissions, automatic upgrades, and even free trips to amazing locations—where I've begun to invest. So it's helped me extend my real-estate holdings internationally.

Becoming a travel agent is simple. I signed up for something called Your Travel Business, or YTB, and presto! I became a travel agent. You can, too. Just go to my special site, www.YTB.com/robertshemin, and sign up. Now you're a Rich Idiot, too.

So book that trip and live rich now. By the way, I should tell you that when you sign up, I get benefits for introducing you. That makes me an even bigger Rich Idiot. But wait—you'll get the same added goodies when you share your travel agent site with your friends and family. Remember, Rich Idiots want others to be rich, too!

Number 2: When Traveling, Ask for an Upgrade

At most resorts or hotels, there are better rooms and bigger rooms with more interesting views, concierge floors with special services, and even luxury suites. When checking in, simply ask if you could be upgraded. Here's how I empower the staff. I say, "If anyone can make this happen, I know it's you." Then I offer them a gift (I often carry chocolates with me), not to bribe them but to brighten their day. You'll be surprised how often a hotel will oblige. Presto! You've just become a Rich Idiot for the duration of your stay!

Number 3: Plan a Group Vacation

Here's one thing I do at least once a year. I put together a group of my friends for a trip or a cruise. This vacation strategy also works very well for school groups, churches, and civic groups. If enough people participate, the airline, the hotel, the resort, or the cruise ship will often give me my trip for free. Not only do I get a fantastic vacation, but I get to spend it with all my friends *and* I get it for free—just for having the idea and putting it together. By the way, Rich Idiots take a portion of the price of the ticket they *would* have paid for but didn't and donate the money to a worthy cause.

Number 4: Swap Houses

I've never done this myself, but my friend Kaye has and she loved it. It's called swapping. Here's how it works: Kaye lived in a great apartment in New York City and wanted to spend a month or so in London. Even though she could afford it, hotels in London are very, very expensive. So she swapped homes. Through one of the many house-swapping Web sites she found a woman with a huge flat in South Kensington who wanted to spend a month in New York. Kaye tells this funny story about her experience:

> I didn't know London, so I really didn't know what kind of neighborhood this woman lived in. She didn't know New York and wasn't sure where I was located. Here's how we solved the geography problem: I told her my apartment was a ten-minute walk from Saks Fifth Avenue, and she told me hers was a ten-minute walk from Harrods! We both felt re-assured. And this turned out to be the most fantastic vacation I've ever had. I kept on paying all my normal New York expenses while I lived in her apartment, and she kept on paying all her normal London housing expenses while she lived in mine. The only personal costs we incurred were for our own phone bills. Not only did this woman share her home, but all her friends came 'round and took me to dinner. They made me feel like a real Londoner, and it cost me ex-actly the same amount as if I'd remained living in my own apartment in New York.

Is Kaye a Rich Idiot, or what? By the way, this swapping can work anywhere around the world. Thousands of people would love to come to your location and offer you theirs in exchange.

6. Savings

Yes, You *Can* Have a Savings Account

I'm not going to tell you to get a second or third job. I'm not going to tell you to give up any of the small pleasures you enjoy or the treats that keep you going. What I am going to tell you is that you've got the beginnings of a pretty substantial savings account already. So let's go find it.

Number 1: Play the "Hunt for Cash" Game

You can't open a new savings account without cash. So we're going to find some cash for you right now. First empty out your change purse and pockets—there's some starter cash right there (and by the way, pennies count). Next go through every pocket of every garment in your closet. I guarantee you'll find more money. Hunt between the sofa cushions. Look on the ledge above the washer or dryer in the laundry room. Check your jewelry box. Go through every single pocketbook and purse you own. Count it up. See? You've had the beginnings of a savings account all along—you just had to know where to look.

You're not done yet. There's more cash just sitting around. Trust me.

Number 2: Have a Garage Sale

Now go through every single room of your house and put a yellow Post-it note on whatever you don't use anymore and can get rid of. Be ruthless. Be firm. Examine your living areas. Your basement. The attic. The garage. If you have a storage area, go through that. Now all those things with all those yellow markers are your second tier of found money. You're going to haul all those things into your front yard or your garage this weekend and have a sale. Don't get crazy greedy. Just get whatever cash you can for all that stuff you never use.

Add that money pile to the first pile. On Monday morning take those two piles of cash to the nearest bank—but make it a new bank, not one that you have accounts in already. And open a savings account.

Done. You've opened a savings account. You've started a new relationship with a future financial friend—the bank. You're on your way!

7. Charity
Yes, You *Can* Give to Charity

"Robert, I don't have enough money for myself and my own family—how can I give to others?" This is the most frequent whine I hear. And here is my response: "I'm going to give you a whole list of ways you can start giving to get like a true Rich Idiot. Just pick one of these and do it!"

Number 1: Give Your Time

Start with one hour of your time. If your hour is worth $5, then that's your charitable contribution. If it's worth $8 or $10 or $100 or even $350, then give that hour to someone who needs it.

- Read to a group of kids in your local hospital or library.
- Dish out dinners in a soup kitchen.
- Volunteer to deliver meals or drive elderly patients to appointments.
- Knit a baby blanket for a clinic.

Number 2: Give Your Skills

Everyone has special skills. Maybe you're a terrific cook. Perhaps you know carpentry or can fix a car. Maybe you love books. How about your computer skills? If you have a skill, volunteer it—that counts as a Rich Idiot charitable donation, too.

- Offer to teach a computer-skills class.
- Offer to teach cooking to unwed mothers.
- Volunteer at a community center and teach mechanics.
- Go to a local church, synagogue, or mosque and offer to help fix stuff.
- Teach an adult literacy class.

Number 3: Give Your Money

Before you begin telling me you have no money, just think about how little it would cost to help others.

- Buy an extra couple of cans of soup when you go grocery shopping. In a month those purchases will add up and you can donate them to a local charity.
- Take your old clothes over to a women's shelter or other group that can get them cleaned and recycled for those in need.
- Add a dollar to every purchase you make and stuff it into one of the charity cans at the checkout counter located in virtually every store in America.
- Buy a sandwich for that homeless person who always hangs out at the end of the street.
- Add 5 percent to the tip for that waitperson who's saving for college.

The "Fake It Till You Make It" Wrap-up

I know it will seem strange at first, but if you do what all other Rich Idiots have done and continue to do—living rich today—you'll most certainly get to live rich tomorrow much faster and with greater satisfaction. Now start practicing the "Fake It Till You Make It" Action Plan.

Your Rich Idiot Upside-Down Action Plan

Follow this plan, starting now, to create the true wealth you desire.

1. Dress up and go out.

Today—right now, in fact—put this book down and go into your closet. Find your best outfit and put it on. Now go to the fanciest restaurant or club in your town. If you can't afford dinner, have just a salad. If you can't afford a salad, sit at the bar and have a soda or a glass of water. Notice the glassware, the table settings, the flowers, the music, the people. See that? You're now one of them. Hold that feeling. Keep it close. It will make you a Rich Idiot soon.

2. Take your dream car for a test-drive.

Walk into the showroom of whatever dealership sells the dream car you aspire to and take it out for a test-drive. Enjoy how it feels, listen to the purr of that engine, smell that new-car leather smell. Now hold that feeling. Keep it close. This car will be yours very soon.

3. Ask for a discount or an upgrade.

Get one discount or upgrade today by asking for it. Ask for a sale price on an item in your local department store. Go to a hotel and ask for an upgrade to a better room. Go into a restaurant and don't take the first table they give you . . . ask for a better one. It may feel awkward at first, but keep practicing. Soon you'll be enjoying all the lifestyle perks of Rich Idiots.

4. Open a special bank account.

Whatever discount or savings you get, put that exact amount into a brand-new savings account called the "Look at Me, I'm a Rich Idiot Account." Now watch how quickly it will grow. That money is your future investment money. That money is money you earned by negotiating. It's money that came to you when you increased your income.

secret no. 5

Rich Idiots Don't Get Rich Alone

*Coming together is a beginning. Keeping together
is progress. Working together is success.*
— HENRY FORD

The Myth of the Individual Success Story

Picture this: It's the final shot of the movie. There he stands—the lone
entrepreneur. The man who single-handedly and against all odds built
a gazillion-dollar empire. The camera captures him tall, proud, and, of
course, tanned; then it pans slowly across a landscape of logos repre-
senting all the brands now under his financial control—until the final
lingering image. There it is, a spinning globe and the tantalizing tease
for the sequel: "He saved the fortunes of a country—can he save the
world?"

America loves this myth. We've loved it from the first time we read
the rags-to-riches stories of Horatio Alger. We've loved it from our
first viewing of *The Lone Ranger.* The myth makes for great drama, but,
of course, it *is* a myth. What *is* true is that not one successful Rich Idiot
ever became successful or successfully rich alone.

And that is one of the most powerful upside-down secrets discovered by Rich Idiots.

Remember!
Rich Idiots didn't get rich all by themselves.

Consider the inventor Thomas Edison. We like to think of him alone, day after day flicking the switch on one failed lightbulb experiment after another. We like to think of him in splendid isolation with only his own will and an occasional cheese sandwich or apple to sustain him. We like to think of him motivating himself in the dark with the now-famous words "I have not failed. I've just found ten thousand ways that won't work." That's the myth.

But check out the Edison reality. Good old Alva had a packed lab—twenty-one assistants and support staff! Isn't that a shock? When asked one day why he employed a team of twenty-one assistants, Edison replied, "If I could solve all the problems myself, I would." He knew that teams are the critical factor in success and that Rich Idiots don't get to be Rich Idiots all by themselves.

Edison isn't the only one who discovered that. A more contemporary example is basketball great Michael Jordan. When describing the importance of teams in sports he said, "Talent wins games, but teamwork . . . wins championships." Even the superstar successful athlete doesn't reach the pinnacle all alone. The team is critical to the success of the individual.

Addressing success in business, management guru Ken Blanchard has said, "None of us is as smart as all of us." In business the team concept can be a make-it-or-break-it proposition. One of the most frequent reasons for the failure of entrepreneurial companies is that the entrepreneur tries to do it all—and fails, often taking his business, his investment, and his dream down the tubes with him. Organizations that enjoy a sharp competitive edge build strong teams and are suspicious of so-called loose cannons—individuals trying to go it alone.

Even one of the most celebrated entrepreneurial successes in American business history, Andrew Carnegie, admitted that "teamwork is the ability to work together toward a common vision. It is the fuel that allows common people to attain uncommon results." And Carnegie was without a doubt the Bill Gates of his century. Now, speaking of Bill Gates . . .

The Bill Gates Solo Act

What do you suppose would happen to Microsoft if Bill Gates did it all himself? Just picture it. There's Bill putting together all those little chips and things that make Windows work. He's writing the text. He's designing the pretty graphics. He's schlepping all over the world to find the best suppliers. Then he's packing those Windows components into boxes and driving those boxes to the post office.

But wait, he's not done yet. He still has to buy ads, take orders, answer e-mails and phone calls, and deal with glitches. Then he has to write checks to pay his suppliers, take his deposits to the bank, and balance his checkbook.

In the middle of all this, he's got to take his kids to school because it's his day to carpool; book a romantic dinner, so he doesn't neglect his spouse; coach Little League; and get the oil in his car changed.

Ridiculous, right? If Bill actually did all this himself, he wouldn't be the Richest Idiot in the World! He'd be a RUB—a very tired RUB like you. There's a lesson here. And yet this is exactly what most entrepreneurs try to do.

A Lesson from Donald Trump

Here's another story that points out the crucial need to recruit help. This one was recently brought home to me by none other than

Donald Trump. We were speaking at the same Learning Annex Wealth Expo, along with other wealth experts. While we were all enjoying a break in the speakers' lounge, a speaker's cell phone rang. He answered it. When he finished his conversation, the Donald went up to him and said, "You don't make enough money." The speaker replied, "Donald, I may not be as wealthy as you, but I'm very well off." Donald remarked, "You don't make enough money; if you did, you wouldn't have to answer your own phone." And it illustrates the main point here: If you attempt to do everything yourself you'll fail. If you use O.P. Power (that's the Power of Other People), you'll succeed.

O.P. Power Separates the RUBs from the Rich Idiots

In the pages that follow you're going to learn exactly how to tap into this major source of Rich Idiot smarts—O.P. Power. You'll learn how to identify, find, and attract O.P.s. You'll learn how to distinguish between true O.P.s and fake ones. You'll learn how to put them into groups for maximum advantage. You'll learn that you need lots and lots of different O.P.s with different goodies to offer you on your journey to riches. You'll learn how to assemble a Dream Team of O.P.s and how to do a quick check to make sure they're going to help you achieve your personal dream.

So don't think that you have to do it all by yourself. In fact, *keep* thinking that way and your splendid isolation will ensure that you'll remain a RUB.

By the way, simply by purchasing this book and letting me in you've added one Robert Shemin to your O.P. team. See, that wasn't so hard, was it?

The Skyscraper Story

Let's say you want to build a big business, create a huge empire. You want lots of wealth. You want to build a monument—perhaps a tall building with your name on the top in lights. You decide the building has to rise one hundred stories and dominate the skyline. Go ahead: Dream big.

But you've never built anything before in your life. So you say, "I want to build a hundred-story building. I don't really know how. I'm not a builder. I'm not a contractor. I'm not a developer, but I'd like to do that." So, how can you make that vision real?

How would a RUB do it? People who still think right side up would probably attempt the whole process themselves. They'd learn how to build, how to deal with codes and zoning. They'd educate themselves about types of construction. They'd take a course on financing. They'd probably learn as much as they could about architecture, building permits, air rights, and all the million and one other details that all have to fit together perfectly for someone to build a building—any building, not just a one-hundred-story high-rise.

Now let's say you're a Rich Idiot who wants to build a hundred-story building. What do you do? You find a builder, a developer, an architect, and experts who specialize in finance. You assemble a team of people who *together* know how to put up that one-hundred-story building and plug in the lights at the top that spell out your name—correctly.

Then what?

Well, you get your team members all working like crazy on this project. Before you know it (this is a *power* team) you've got your hundred-story building—the biggest in your city. And it's even named after you. At the ribbon-cutting ceremony, you're reading your speech and naturally thanking this incredibly long list of people who "made it happen."

So here's the multimillion-dollar question: When did the building actually get built? Did it get built when the architect drew the plans, or when the city approved the zoning, or when the first shovelful of earth was lifted out of the site, or when the foundations were poured, or when the lights were turned on, or when that ribbon was cut?

Remember!
It's the acorn, dummy—not the oak.

I'll tell you when that building was first built. The instant *you* first thought of it. And that's the second part of the O.P. secret. True, Rich Idiots never get rich alone—but the idea, the dream, the vision belongs first and always to the visionary, to the Rich Idiot who wanted to make it real and recruited others to help turn an idea into reality.

So for you to become very wealthy and very successful, where does it start and where does it end? With the idea of you becoming that wealthy successful person. Right?

Remember!
The Rich Idiot makes the spark;
Other People make the blaze.

Robert "Before O.P.": A True Story

Still not convinced? Here's what my life looked like *before* I learned the O.P. Power secret.

Several years ago, when I was starting my own wealth journey, I began investing in real estate—my first Rich Idiot pathway. Things went fairly well at first. I was buying properties. I was applying for financing. I was doing the bookkeeping. I was my own leasing agent. I was putting together teams of contractors—you could say I was my own general contractor. I was also doing the property inspections, selling properties, attending all the closings—everything.

Sure, my business grew steadily but my personal life was in chaos. I was working too hard, so my personal life suffered, my family life suffered, my spiritual life was not where it should be. And the strangest part was that even though I was working all the time, I wasn't making a ton of money. Even my weekends were filled with business, because whenever I took a Saturday off I'd spend it worrying about all the stuff I hadn't finished on Friday. And when I took a Sunday off, I'd spend it worrying about all the stuff that was waiting for me Monday morning.

What's more, I felt tired, cranky, and fearful that I'd make a lot of mistakes that would cost me my hard-earned money. The point is that I was trying to do everything.

What happened? I got some really good advice and took it. What was the advice? It's the same advice I'm giving you in this chapter: *Don't do it all alone.*

After I took that advice to heart I found a bunch of people to help me. I hired a management company to help manage my properties. I hired a contractor to deal with all the repairs and tradesmen. I got a bookkeeper to pay the bills, make the deposits, and balance my checkbook. In addition to paying these people, I made them my partners in a small way, giving them some ownership in the success of the enterprise. The bigger the business grew, the wealthier we'd all become.

Remember!
Pigs get fat. Hogs get slaughtered. Let others
make money, too. Don't be too greedy.

Rich Idiots always share with those O.P.s who helped them make it. *Always.* Ask yourself if you share what you make with those who help you make it, or if you hog your income and revenue. When you make "partners" in wealth of all those who help you earn, save, create, and build, your riches will increase dramatically. Incentives stimulate others to do their best for you, because by helping you these people are also helping themselves become richer. And the huge wheel of wealth keeps turning.

When I realized the power of turning Other People into my wealth partners, I turned a major money corner, and I've never looked back.

The result? I tripled my income! What's more important, I had precious time to spend with my family and friends. I was able to take care of my own physical, intellectual, and spiritual needs. I got back my life. I got back my soul!

So listen up. I hereby make you the CEO of your life. You generate the ideas and the passion; others will help make your dreams come true.

This is one of the biggest secrets of Rich Idiots. The minute you turn your thinking upside down and trust O.P. Power, the magic begins to happen.

How to Tap into the Magic of O.P. Power

As you sit and read this book, are you feeling all alone? You're probably thinking, "*How* can I ever become a Rich Idiot? *How* is it ever going to happen for me? I have so much to do. *How* can I get it all done?" Listen to me. You don't have to know how to do it all by yourself. Let me emphasize this again: You can make your wildest wealth dreams come true and become a Rich Idiot yourself through the magic of O.P. Power.

Start by doing three things to accelerate and ensure your success:

1. Get rid of O.P.s who *want* you to remain a RUB.
2. Find O.P.s who *want* you to become a Rich Idiot.
3. Build your own O.P. Dream Team.

Three Types of O.P.s

There are three types of O.P.s. The first is the Toxics, who you'll want to get rid of as fast as you can. The second is the Enablers, who are already Rich Idiots. The third type will compose your Dream Team. From this moment forward, anytime you get advice from anyone, evaluate that advice by putting the adviser into one of these categories:

- The Toxics
- The Enablers
- The Dream Team

The Toxics

This category can be tough, because it often contains people who mean a lot to us—including family and friends. You can love them, but unless they're experts or Rich Idiots themselves, *never* listen to any advice they give you. The Toxics show up in the following five subcategories.

1. The "I Mean Well" Group

These Toxic people have absolutely no idea what they're talking about. Unfortunately, most people get some, if not all, of their wealth advice from the "I Mean Well" group. For example, your second cousin who's a greeter at a discount department store loves to tell you how investing in the stock market will never work. What's his reasoning? Because he never did it himself. People are programmed to tell you you'll never do a certain thing because they themselves have never done that thing.

Let me ask you this: Would you take your child to get an eye operation from a foot surgeon? Of course not. Why? Duh! Because a foot surgeon knows about feet, not eyes. Pay no attention to all those people in this category—the ones who love to give you "expert" advice without ever having followed the advice they so liberally dish out. Find out if these well-meaning people just "talk the talk" without "walking the walk." If it turns out they have never done anything to become a Rich Idiot themselves, *never* take any advice from them.

2. The "Tried It and Failed" Group

The second type in the Toxic category includes that unhappy bunch of folks who have tried to become Rich Idiots and failed. This is where most people get their next big chunk of wealth advice from. The "Tried It and Failed" crowd often contains people who made bad decisions in real estate or in the stock market or who started a business that crashed and burned. Now they feel qualified to give you tons of advice about these investment vehicles. The minute you confide your wealth dreams to such people they jump in and proceed to tell you their personal horror stories. *Do not listen.* In fact, *run away* as fast as you possibly can. The law of attraction (which you'll read about next) works incredibly well. If you stay close to those who keep experiencing money failures, you could fail, too. An analogy may help illustrate what I'm talking about. My friend Doug, who's been divorced five times and is now hitched to wife number six, loves giving out relationship advice. But after failing repeatedly to learn from failure, he's not going to find me very interested in his pearls of wisdom.

3. The "Comfort Zone" Group

The third group of Toxics is made up of the buddies you hang out with because you feel comfortable in their company. These are the folks with whom you go to ball games, drink beer, share barbecues, and work beside. They could be old school buddies, favorite cousins, the guy who gave you a great deal on your car, or your next-door neighbors. They live in the same kind of house as you, shop in the same stores, eat in the same restaurants, go to the same movies, and make about the same money. That last one—make about the same money—can kill your Rich Idiot goal. In fact, it's the main reason to stay away from their advice in money matters.

To understand why, you'll need to take a short test. It will show you how wealthy you *really* are right now and how much your "Comfort Zone" friends limit your financial growth. It can be a major wake-up call for wannabe Rich Idiots.

Start by taking a survey of the five people you spend the most time with. Try to get them to be honest about their income and net worth, then average those two sets of numbers. I'm guessing that the figures you get will be close to your own income and net worth. What does this tell you? People around us influence the level of wealth we attain. So change the people in your circle and you'll change your wealth profile. How? Coming up is a guide to changing your own wealth image. This, in turn, will help you find and feel more comfortable around wealthier friends—a major step on your Rich Idiot staircase.

Remember!
Hang out with Rich Idiots and you'll get rich.
Hang out with RUBs and you'll stay a RUB.

---

4. The Dream Stealers

We're products of our environment. We have to be wary of the influences swirling around us. As you begin your journey to riches, be careful to protect yourself from the Dream Stealers—the negative people in your life. I've discovered them among my friends and family. The writer Gore Vidal once said, "Whenever a friend succeeds, a little something in me dies." Run away from this type of person as fast as you can.

You probably have such people in your life right now. The minute you try to do something different—start a new business, invest in a new stock, do something or anything to improve your wealth—what do these killjoys say? Nothing positive, certainly. Rather, you get lots of dire warnings about imminent disaster.

When I first got into real estate, several family members were absolutely against it. They thought investing was too risky. They thought I didn't have the skills. They thought I would fail and embarrass them. But I discovered the real motivation behind their comments. All their negativity had nothing to do with me. The Dream Stealers were really talking about themselves.

Be warned. The more successful you become, the more the Dream Stealers will try to pull you back. You may even lose good friends and loved ones in the process. But remember, they'll find themselves left behind because of their own fear and failure, not your success.

There's a wonderful story that Bruce Springsteen tells about how even though he's recorded a number of best-selling albums and performed to sellout crowds, his own mother still tells him, "Bruce, you've never finished college. You should go back and get a degree. This rock-and-roll thing may not work out." Bruce loves his mother dearly, but is *she* the best person to be giving him advice on wealth and success?

5. The "Ouch, It's Me" Group

This exclusive group contains only one member: you. The final Toxic person you need to watch out for is yourself. If you're a RUB who still thinks right side up, still repeats the same patterns that keep you working hard and staying broke, get out of your own way. Put this book down and go stand in front of a mirror. What do you see? Do you see a Toxic person—your own worst enemy, that evil twin always whispering in your ear that you're a failure? Or do you see a cheerleader?

Turn your thinking upside down so you can become a Rich Idiot.

The Enablers

There are four main O.P. groups in the Enabler category.

1. *The OPE Group.* This group will offer their experience—hence my term: Other People's Experience. Most mentors belong in this category.
2. *The OPI Group.* These are the partners and experts who will share with you their ideas—or, as I like to call them, Other People's Ideas.

3. *The OPT Group.* These folks will make it possible for you to use your precious time to do only those things you alone can do. Meanwhile, they'll give their own time to assist you in your goals. This is the beauty of leverage. Let other people do what they do best so you can do what you do best.

4. *The OPM Group.* This very important group will put up the money you need to reach your own goals.

Each of these groups accelerates your progress by providing must-have wealth tools: experience, ideas, time, or money. Why? Because of the laws of attraction and influence.

Now, in sketching out the sort of people who will help and the sort who will hinder, I'm not telling you to get different friends or drop your family. I'm telling you to be aware of their influence on you. If you want to be a Rich Idiot and make more money and be happier, you have to hang around people who are already Rich Idiots, make lots of money, and are happy with their lives.

Remember!
The influence of Other People can be sludge
in your rocket fuel—or accelerant.

Success depends not only on what you do but also on who you do it with—who you know. I'm not talking about favors or connections. I'm talking about *influence*. If I hang out with people who drink beer all day and night, chances are I'll drink beer day and night, too. If I hang around people who drink water and jog every morning, chances are I'll drink water and jog, too. So ask the tough question: "Who am I hanging around and how much are they holding me back?"

Let's examine each of the Enabler groups—people you want in your life!

OPE: Mentors

I never knew a Rich Idiot who didn't have at least one OPE mentor—and many Rich Idiots (including me) have a whole bunch who lend their experience. What's an OPE mentor? Well, he or she is that part of your OPE wealth-building kit that relies on Other People's Experience. Someone once described a mentor as a person whose hindsight can become your foresight. Mentors can make sure you aren't reinventing the wheel. They can share personal lessons that will dramatically shorten your own learning curve. They can reduce your risk of failure and increase your chances for success. But the most important reason to have a mentor is this: They're your inspiration; they're your beacon. After all, *they've* become successful and so can *you!*

How do you find your OPE mentors? It can seem hard at first, but seek out someone who is doing what you want to do. Look for people who are accomplished at making money in the exact field that lights your fire. And when you find them, just ask them to share information with you once a month or so. Take them out to lunch. Buy them a cup of coffee. Tell them you admire their accomplishments and want to emulate them. Show them that you aspire to become wealthy and successful and that, having reached your goals, you'll become a mentor yourself one day.

You'll find that most Rich Idiots *love* to share ideas and help others. So don't be shy. Just step right up and find an OPE mentor or two.

Robert's True Story

Let me tell you the story of when I first tuned in to the power of Other People and got some mentoring that would change my life.

I was just another guy, working in a huge corporation and helping other people grow their money. Then one day a new world of possibilities opened up.

My boss sent me to visit prospective clients who reportedly had a "ton of money," the goal being to sign them up for financial-planning services. When I arrived at their office I thought I had the wrong address. I found myself outside a ramshackle structure—more like a trailer than a building. I saw only one vehicle in the parking lot—a dented and dirty blue pickup truck. I immediately thought, "This can't be right. Either the plumber's here or these folks are broke."

But just to make sure, I went inside. The things I saw from the doorway didn't look any more promising. Lots of junk lying around, broken doors, a busted window, and misshapen pieces of wood. And then a door opened and a man walked in. I didn't know it then, but he was the first Rich Idiot I'd ever met and he would become the first O.P. to help me become a Rich Idiot, too. About seventy-five years old, this guy wore a shabby pair of overalls splotched with paint and looked like Jed Clampett's poor cousin from the old *Beverly Hillbillies* TV show. He greeted me warmly and invited me into his "office." I looked around, even more shocked at what I was seeing or, rather, what I *wasn't* seeing. Dusty files covered every surface. A big jar of pencils sat on a wooden desk next to an old-fashioned black phone. No signs of technology— no computer, no printer, no cell phone—nothing that resembled what my boss had described as a "lucrative account." He asked his wife to join us—and she didn't look the part of a wealthy client, either.

But my sales training kicked in; I straightened my executive tie, and, not wanting to appear rude, I began to talk to him and his wife about financial planning. All the time I was talking, though, I was convinced that someone had played a practical joke on me. To me it was clear by how they dressed and the state of their truck and their office that they possessed little money, certainly not enough to need our high-end financial-planning services.

So after about thirty minutes of talking to them, I thanked them for their time and attention and exited the office. "What a waste of my time," I thought as I got back into my car and started the engine. But something told me not to drive away. And so, trusting my instincts, I turned off the engine, got out of my car, and knocked on the door again. The same scruffy old man opened it and said, "Robert, I thought you left."

"I was going to," I replied, "but I forgot to ask you one question. You're very nice people, but what do you do here—what do you do for a living among all this junk?"

Remember!
Find your Rich Idiot moment.

Please take a few seconds to sit back in your chair, breathe deeply, and think about a single moment in your life where everything changed—everything turned upside down, and, consequently, your life was never the same again. Perhaps it was when you changed careers, or moved across the country, or held your first child in your arms for the very first time. Whatever it was, you now look back on it and realize it was your defining moment, the exact instant your life took a new direction.

That's what happened to me that hot Nashville afternoon. Going back inside that shack of an office changed my life.

"Come here, son," the man said. "I'm not smart like you. I never even graduated from high school. My wife and I did something most people won't do. We worked hard for the first few years. Now, let me show you something." Then he opened up an old accounting book and, running his finger down the rows of figures, gave me my very first Rich Idiot lesson. He showed me how twenty years back he was a RUB. But there was a small property up the street from his that was going into foreclosure. So he scraped together every dime he had, bought it, fixed it up a bit, and sold it. He showed me in that old ledger how he made a few dollars on that first property. He took that small investment and bought another house, fixed it up, and sold it for a small profit. He did this over and over for five long years. He and his wife painted, scraped, and cleaned. They dug and planted. And then

instead of selling the houses they'd worked so hard to fix up, he started
to rent them out. As the man turned the last ledger page, I saw that he
and his wife owned 120 properties. And they owned them "free and
clear," with each bringing in rental income that allowed them to make
over $1 million a year.

That's the money part. They were also spending six months a year
traveling around, enjoying themselves. That's the time part. This couple had created the perfect life—they had money *and* they had time.
They were Rich Idiots!

What did I do? I closed that ledger and asked that man to help me,
to teach me, to share his secrets with me. And he did. The rest, as they
say, is history.

From that moment forward I asked others to help me. Without
exception they did, each taking me closer to my perfect life and to the
cashing of my own wealth check. Today, as you read this book, remember that you're not alone, either. Let me be the first to help you.

But next, let me show you how to find others. Because one of the
smartest things I ever learned was that I could never become a Rich
Idiot alone—and neither can you!

OPI: Footsteps Group

Tremendous opportunities abound for becoming a Rich Idiot. People
sometimes say to me, "Robert, I want to become a Rich Idiot, but I
don't have any idea what to do. I don't have a business or investment
idea. I don't know where I should start." Here's how I reply: "No problem. Join a footsteps group and plug into OPI—Other People's Ideas."

You don't have to come up with your own ideas for wealth. Lots of
other people have come up with wealth-creating ideas and are more
than willing to share them with you. There are people who will help
you start your own business. There are great business ideas all ready to
go, many where the creator just needs a partner. There are "businesses
in a box" all set up, with proven and viable models and support systems

built in. I often tell people, "Instead of starting from scratch, which is very challenging, find others who've already done much of the heavy lifting and see if you can work with them."

Follow Footsteps

Let me tell you about some mistakes I made before I became a Rich Idiot. I joined a sales organization and thought, "This is a piece of cake. I'm going to get rich just doing nothing." Well, I did nothing, and nothing happened. Then I thought, "I can figure out how to do this." So I spent almost a year working up my own systems. Everyone at the company warned me against trying to figure out my own get-rich method. They told me over and over they'd been in the business for ten, twenty, even thirty years and they knew the way to get rich. But I was convinced that I could find a better way. The result? A whole year of potential wealth wasted and no money coming in.

Then I did what a Rich Idiot would have done in the first place. I sought out the most successful person in the company and said, "Tell me exactly what you did to get rich in this business and I'll do the same thing." He gave me a thirty-line script.

"You've got to be kidding," I told him. "Is this all I have to do? It sounds too easy."

He replied, "Do you want to be successful or not?"

Of course I did. So I wrote down what he told me to say to prospective clients and followed it word for word. All of a sudden my income went from $10 a week to $500 a week to $5,000 a week! And what had I learned? I'd learned to use another person's business ideas and follow in his footsteps to wealth.

Since then I've discovered that you can use OPIs in lots of other ways. For example, I used to do all my own accounting. Then I found a terrific accountant who not only took over all the bookkeeping (which I hated and wasn't very good at) but at tax time actually saved me thousands of dollars. Not only did I use OPIs (his ideas on tax savings) and OPE (his experience in doing accounting for real-estate entrepreneurs like me) but I added a major dollar amount to my own net worth. He made me a Richer Idiot!

OPT: The Time Wizards

What's the most precious commodity you have? If you said money, you're wrong. You can always make more money. The right answer is, of course, time. You can't make more time. So any time you can save should be considered a precious gift. If you aspire to become a true Rich Idiot, focus on the time your riches can buy. Learn to use OPT (Other People's Time).

The following true story brings my point home. A guy named Jeff came to one of my real-estate seminars several years ago. At the time he was a salesman selling frozen-food products and was making around $43,000 a year. He was married and had three kids.

"I want to get into investing, Robert," he told me, "not because of the money so much, but because I want more time to spend with my family. Right now, I travel a lot—I'm on the road practically five days a week, and I don't get to see my wife or my children nearly enough. If I worked for myself, I could work from home and not miss any precious family moments."

So I taught this food salesman how to invest in real estate. In about a year, he'd replaced his salary with income from investments. I liked him and I respected his family values. We became friends. Over the next couple of years his income soared to $300,000 a year and kept right on climbing. He and his family were set for life. And then tragedy struck. He called me one day in tears.

"My wife has just been diagnosed with liver cancer," he said, sobbing. "She's only thirty-nine and has four weeks left to live." And then a small miracle happened. Because of this man's wealth he was able to buy his wife experimental drugs that cost $25,000 a week, which the insurance company would not pay for. With that medication he bought her a precious three extra months. With those drugs his children had a mother for ninety more days. This man's wealth bought an extra measure of time. And that's what money can do. The question for all of us is, What is a weekend or ninety days with a loved one worth? The answer is, It's priceless.

Buying Other People's Time

Think of life as a grocery store. You want a salad. Does that mean you have to grow the lettuce, tomatoes, and onions yourself? Press the olive oil? Bottle the vinegar? Carve the salad bowl? No, of course not. You go to the store and you buy what you need.

The same principle applies when you buy other people's time for a wealth-growing enterprise. Of course, I always try to make the revenues lead the expenses.

You need sales. Hire a salesperson.
You need filing. Hire a file clerk.
You need a brochure. Hire a writer and a graphic artist.
You need a Web site. Hire a Web developer.
You need bills paid. Hire a bookkeeper.
You need orders taken. Hire an order taker.
You need errands run. Hire a personal assistant.
You need housework done. Hire a cleaner.
You need dinner. Order takeout.
You need child care. Hire a nanny or a babysitter.
You need clothes. Get a personal shopper.

You get the idea. Think of the dozens of tasks you can use other people's time to accomplish while you use your precious time to become a Rich Idiot.

Still not convinced? Okay, let me ask you this: "What's your time worth right now? Do you make $10 an hour? Or $20 an hour? Or $100 an hour?" Now try this: If you make $10 an hour, find someone to help you with one of your tasks for $5 an hour. Your neighbor's kid, for example. Guess what? You've just saved $5 every hour. Now go put that $5 toward your investments and use that hour to make $100 more!

OPM: Show Me the Money!

Every Rich Idiot knows (especially when first starting out) that to get rich faster you must use OPM (Other People's Money). We all did it. Every single "self-made" wealthy person you see in the media started out broke and used OPM to build the foundations of their fortune.

The only warning I issue here is that if you think it's bad to lose your own money, believe me, it's worse to lose someone else's. So be very careful. But don't shy away from the OPM opportunity. Don't be a frightened, overcautious RUB.

So how do you get other people to give you their money when you don't have any of your own? No problem.

First, you need a terrific idea for a way to make money for yourself, and you have to get really excited about it. You have to believe with every fiber of your being that this idea will make you incredibly wealthy. Got that? Good.

Next, you have to write down exactly how that idea is going to make you rich. By writing it down you make it real. This is your plan for monetizing your idea. Write down how much it will cost to get started. How much it will cost to build it up for the first three months, six months, a year. Write down how much money your idea can bring in and when. That's it. Now you are ready for OPM.

How I Got $1 Million Without Asking

Asking for money from others is pretty stressful, so make up your mind to get all the financing you need *without* asking for it. Don't laugh. I did it, and so can you.

Here's what I did. I found an amazing deal on a large real-estate investment. I cranked out the numbers. I checked them and double-checked them. I knew this was a winner. But I needed a million dollars to make my plan happen. I didn't have a million dollars at the time, not even close to a million. So I took my idea around to a bunch of banks, and all I got was a polite no.

I needed a different strategy. So I decided to visit banks and *not* ask for money. I decided to ask for advice instead. I'd let my idea do the talking. I put on my Rich Idiot outfit and went to my local bank manager.

"Mr. Bank Manager," I said, "I know how busy you are, but I was wondering if I could have a few minutes of your time. I don't want any money, but I'd welcome your advice." Believe me, many people can't resist giving advice.

"No problem," he said. "What can I advise you on?"

Great, I thought. *The first part of my plan worked. I've got the banker's attention.*

Next I showed him my plan on paper. "I'm just starting out but I think I've found something really profitable. Can you look over these figures and tell me what you think?"

While he was looking at the paper I told him my goal was to create low-income affordable housing. I showed him a few photos of the property as it looked now and sketches of what it would look like once I fixed it up. Remember, I was only asking for advice, not money.

He put down the plan and excused himself. "I'll be right back," he said.

Ten minutes later he returned with a couple of other bank people, who introduced themselves as the heads of commercial lending, residential lending, and private banking. "Robert's got a great business plan here," said my first banker (who's now my good friend). "How can we get him funding?"

That's not the end of the story. A RUB would say, "Yay!" and sign whatever papers these bankers offered up, just to close the deal. But a Rich Idiot would thank the bankers politely, roll up his sheaf of papers, take away all his pretty photos and drawings, and say, "Thank you very much. Let me think about it for a few days." Then that Rich Idiot would go across the street to a rival bank. He'd ask to see the manager, and here's what he'd say: "Hi, Mr. Bank Manager, I need your advice. Bank XYZ across the street just offered to fund my million-dollar real-estate deal, but I'm not sure if I should accept it. I thought I'd get a second opinion." That's exactly what I did. It didn't take long for Bank Manager No. 2 to offer me funding, too, and at a better rate.

Wait. This million-dollar story isn't over yet. I went back to the first bank. "Mr. First Banker, now I really have a problem and I need your help," I confessed. "Bank ABC across the street just offered to fund this project. Here's the offer. Can you tell me what I should do?" This is a no-brainer. The first bank manager didn't just match the second bank manager's offer; he bested it. I got my funding. And I've been with that bank for more than twelve years.

See what happens when you ask for OPM?

But this story isn't just about raising money. It's one of my best illustrations of the power of turning your thinking upside down. When I mention this story in my seminars I often get some very upset RUBs challenging me. Here's a sampling of what they say: "Shouldn't you have been direct with the first bank and simply asked for a loan? Shouldn't you have taken the first loan when it was offered and not risked the relationship by going to a competing bank? Why did you need a second loan offer? Weren't you afraid you'd get both banks upset and end up with no money at all?"

My answer is simple: Don't be a RUB. Be an upside-down-thinking Rich Idiot. What was the worst that could have happened? I would have been in the same position as when I started—looking for money. What did happen? I found not one but two major players to fund my venture and add to my O.P. list.

Stop being afraid. Stop following the rules that haven't made you rich yet. Start living large by expanding your network of contacts, information, and potential. Go ahead. Take a risk. Be bolder than you think you are. Be a Rich Idiot.

Your OPM Kit Should Contain:

- A great moneymaking idea
- A written plan that you've checked over and over
- A Rich Idiot outfit so you look successful
- A carefully rehearsed script, so that you don't miss any points but still sound natural
- A list of lots of sources for OPM

Rich Idiots are creative. They don't just rely on banks or lending institutions for their OPM, and neither should you. Look to successful people you know: business owners; professionals such as accountants and financial planners; relatives; and friends. If you're buying a property or a business, the present owner(s) may help you finance the purchase. Think outside the "bank box" and you will find lots of sources of Other People's Money just waiting for you to come along.

Your Dream Team

Your dream team is the third way to use O.P. Power to help make you a Rich Idiot. The first question most RUBs ask me is "Robert, why do I need a team? I can do a lot of the stuff myself, especially at the beginning."

Wrong. It's at the beginning *especially* that you need a Dream Team. Your wealth journey starts when you're the most inexperienced and vulnerable. Your risk of failure at the start is great. Your Dream Team can protect you and help you overcome the wealth-building obstacles that may arise.

Patrick Seitz wrote an interesting article in *Investor's Business Daily* showing what a new entrepreneur can achieve with the help of seasoned experts. Let me share a few lines with you.

"A successful team requires the right balance of diversity and cohesion," says Brian Uzzi, associate professor of management and organizations at Northwestern's Kellogg School of Management. "Diversity is reflected in new collaborations while cohesion comes from repeat collaborations," he says.

Robert's Rules for Building Your Dream Team

1. Use referrals.

Remember, I said you should find a mentor or ask other Rich Idiots for help and advice. Fellow Rich Idiots can be extremely helpful. They've already located the best lawyer, the best accountant, the best tax person, the best sources for practically everything you'd ever need to build your own wealth. Ask for and use their referrals.

2. Don't be cheap.

I learned this one the hard way. I know you're just starting out and you want to save money. But undercompensating your Dream Team members is *not* the way to go. Your team needs to be the best of the best. They're saving you money. They're making you money. They're protecting you. This is not an area where you should be pressing for bargains.

3. Make sure your advisers are experts.

Even with referrals you still have to do your own homework. If you want an attorney who can help with your business, make sure he or she has other business clients; the same goes for a lawyer you want to use for real estate. Apply the same "Are you an expert in this field?" litmus test to everyone on your team. You aren't paying people to learn; you're paying them to perform.

4. Use an association.

Business Network International (BNI) is the world's largest business referral organization, and joining can result in getting great mentors, making terrific strategic alliances, and getting closer to becoming a Rich Idiot.

So what have I been saying in this chapter? Yes, it bears repeating. By turning your "I can do this all by myself" thinking upside down and joining forces with amazing people, you can use their experience, ideas, time, and money to become a Rich Idiot faster and smarter.

And Now, Ladies and Gentlemen . . .

Abraham Lincoln once said, "Things may come to those who wait, but only the things left by those who hustle." So what are you waiting for? Keep reading and get going on the next action plan.

Your Rich Idiot Upside-Down Action Plan

Starting now, follow this plan to create the true wealth you desire.

1. Make a Rich Idiot O.P. list. On a sheet of paper, make a list of all the people you know who could offer you:
   a) their experience
   b) their ideas
   c) their time
   d) their money
2. Write down the specific types of people you want to compose your own Dream Team (e.g., lawyer, accountant, and so on) and list places where you can find them.
3. Need help? Go to www.GetRichWithRobert.com for lists that can help you—lending sources, professional services, and more.

part THREE

FIRE

s e c r e t   n o .   6

It's All About Your Assets

*Becoming wealthy is like playing Monopoly . . . the person
who can accumulate the most assets wins the game.*
— NOEL WHITTAKER

Cut to the Chase

You only need one thing to be a Rich Idiot. If you've got it, you're a Rich
Idiot. If you don't, you're a RUB. Can you guess what that one thing is?

- A luxury rental on South Beach next door to Robert and his
  friends
- A brand-new car that valets always park right outside the door of
  the restaurant
- So many designer clothes you have to convert two rooms into a
  closet
- A private limo and driver to whisk you around when you don't
  feel like driving
- Your very own table at the best restaurant in town whenever you
  get the munchies
- Decorator-selected everything, from your sofa to your commode

If you picked even one of these items, tempting though they are, you're in RUB-land. Do not pass Go. Do not collect *any* money. Why? Because none of these are even remotely close to the one thing that makes Rich Idiots rich, and that's assets.

Stay with me now. This is one of the most important secrets you'll ever learn about wealth and how it is created.

Upside Down and On Your Assets

You're probably thinking you're going to get rich when you start making more money. And to you that means getting a raise, getting another job, winning the lottery. Understand this: All these things may make you rich, but they won't make you a Rich Idiot. Why? Because Rich Idiots don't make money by working a job, depending on a raise, working two jobs, or even winning lotteries. Rich Idiots get rich only one way: They quit their job. They quit their second job. They tear up their lottery ticket and they go out and buy assets—and many Rich Idiots don't even use a dime of their own money to do it. Got that? You don't need a job. You don't need a windfall. You don't even need any money to start on your Rich Idiot asset-acquisition plan. You're probably thinking right now that you need a lot of money to start investing. Wrong. Most multimillionaire investors started with less than $1,000! Keep reading. I'll show you how you can start with as little as $100 or, better yet, no money of your own at all!

What's an Asset?

Robert's Rule for determining what is and isn't an asset is simple: An asset is anything that makes you money. And owning at least one is the only true way to become a really happy, successful Rich Idiot. Too simple a definition for you? Here's one from a financial dictionary; it's formal but it basically says the same thing: "a resource having economic value that an individual, corporation or country owns or controls with the expectation that it will provide future benefit."

Remember when you were in the science lab at high school and you got to dissect some creature and look at its parts under a microscope? Let's do the same with this thing called an asset.

First you should know that all true assets share these three characteristics:

1. They have value.
2. You own or control them.
3. They provide you with future benefit (a.k.a. money).

Rich Idiots check off each of these essentials before they buy anything. And when Rich Idiots buy, they buy assets first. This makes them more successful and much wealthier than RUBs, who buy liabilities, or the evil twin of assets.

What's a Liability?

According to Dictionary.com, liabilities are "moneys owed; debts or pecuniary obligations." That's to the point. But I like this definition from Answers.com even better: A liability is "something for which one is liable; an obligation, responsibility or debt and something that holds one back; a handicap."

The Good Twin (Assets) vs. the Evil Twin (Liabilities)

It's true that both assets and liabilities have value. In that respect, they're the same. It's also true that you own or control assets, and because you're responsible for your liabilities, that's a type of ownership as well—although I might add that more often it feels like liabilities own *you*.

Now let's look at the future. Assets provide you with future bene-fits, such as money in the form of income or cash. Liabilities, on the other hand, take money away from you; they "hold you back"; they're a "handicap."

Remember!
Buy assets first because they *bring* you money.
Buy liabilities second because they *cost* you money.

Let's go back a couple of pages to the list of goodies and toys and go through them. Now that you have a solid definition of assets, you'll be able very quickly to see why these are definitely *not* assets.

- *A luxury rental on South Beach next door to Robert and his friends*

If you own this condo, or have a lease option on it, then it could become an asset. Real estate is one of the major assets Rich Idiots love to acquire. But as long as you're a tenant, this asset is a liability—for you, not for the owner. Every month you spend your money on the rent, all you get back is a cool view and an address that will impress your friends. Moreover, when you move out, you can't convert the condo to cash. So there's no doubt it's a liability and not an asset. By the way, Robert and his friends who live on South Beach own their condos or have lease options on them, making their apartments assets. Get the difference?

- *A brand-new car that valets always park right outside the door of the restaurant*

If you plunked down $80,000 or $85,000 for this brand-new, really cool car and drove it out of the showroom, you probably lost about $25,000. Wow. That makes this car you're so proud of a big lia-bility and most decidedly not an asset. Go back to the definition. Sure the car has value. Of course, you own it, or at least control it (probably along with your partner, the bank, or the finance com-pany), but no matter how cool, these wheels will not bring you future cash. Cars are not assets. A rare exception would be if you bought a classic car and owned it for a time and then sold it for more than what you'd paid. Then that car would have been an asset. See the difference?

- *So many designer clothes you have to convert two rooms into a closet*

Clothes do have value. They make you look hot and feel good, and if they're the work of certain designers they confer status. So in that sense they're an asset. In your closet or on your "bod," there's no ques-tion you own or at least control them—another indicator of an asset. But here's the catch: Clothes lose their value as soon as you snip off the tags. And that makes them a liability. Again, there can be an exception. Here's one: If you bought Jacqueline Kennedy's Halston-designed pink pillbox hat, that would be an asset—because it would have gone up in price. Why? Because the hat is no longer just a hat, it's a col-lectible—and collectibles, like art, antiques, vintage clothing, and coins, can be very good assets.

- *A private limo and driver to whisk you around when you don't feel like driving*

The limo is not an asset because it's something you have to pay for. It's money coming out of your pocket with no hope of future replen-ishment. Ditto for the driver.

- *Your very own table at the best restaurant in town whenever you get the munchies*

This item is one of the ultimate status symbols. Perhaps it's the round table by the window at Michael's, a trendy restaurant in New York, or a seat at Tony Soprano's table in the Badda Bing. The bowing and scraping that greets a favored regular is great for the ego, but it's not an asset. That best seat in the house will cost you—and that makes it a liability.

- *Decorator-selected everything, from your sofa to your commode*

Top-of-the-line decor is great, but when the next "in vogue" decorator comes on the scene all those beautiful furnishings (from couches to commodes and from draperies to divans) turn into just secondhand stuff, fetching much less in the consignment market than they did when you first bought them. Looks great, but no assets here, except if your furnishings are bona fide antiques. Then we're back to collectibles.

RUBs and Rich Idiots: Who Acquires What?

RUBs tend to acquire liabilities (consumables), which is a surefire way to identify a RUB, while Rich Idiots acquire assets, which is what makes them rich in the first place.

Take a close look at this list. Where do you fit? Do you own such assets as cash in a savings account, CDs, or mutual funds? How about real estate? Or a stock portfolio? Hopefully you're not tossing all your money at flashy cars, clothes, and furniture, or frittering it away by constantly dining at four-star restaurants and taking luxury vacations.

RUBs	Rich Idiots
Cars	Cash
Furniture	Real estate
Clothes	Stock portfolio
Trips	Businesses

The Two Most Secret Rich Idiot Assets

There are two more assets Rich Idiots hold very dear, and they're just as important in growing wealth as cash, real estate, stock portfolios, or ownership of a business. The first is "you"; the second is "your time."

This is a big upside-down moment. *You're* your most important asset. Your time is your next-most-important asset. How are you treating those two assets?

Your Time and Your Money

Most people trade their hours for dollars. You've got a job and you put in your eight, or ten, or even eighteen hours. What do you get? Money. What have you done? You've just traded your time for money. And it's very hard to get wealthy that way. You're basically turning yourself into a liability when you do that. Why?

Because you have only a limited amount of time to trade for dollars. At some point you're going to run out. Maybe you've reached that moment already. No time left and your pile of dollars isn't growing as an asset would grow. Rather, it's diminishing as a liability diminishes.

That's the time part. Now let's talk about the "you" part.

I got very disturbed once during a seminar. I asked the audience, about 25,000 people, "How many of you with jobs can't wait to get to work on Monday morning?" Up until that moment I'd been joking and kidding with the group, and they'd been laughing and full of energy. Then I saw the result of my question. I was shocked. Only three people put up their hands. Can you imagine, given the size of that audience, getting only three positive responses? It was so quiet. It sounded like a library or a morgue. Nobody was smiling anymore. The mood had changed. Something like 24,997 people were apparently trading themselves—their most valuable Rich Idiot asset—for a job they disliked and for time they resented spending. Here's the irony: Those three hadn't heard the question correctly. I had asked, "How many of you with a job . . ." All three worked for themselves.

One traded stocks and had built up a sizable portfolio over several years. The second had been buying and selling real estate part-time for the past four years, and her houses were now bringing in enough money that she could quit her job and do real estate full-time. The third person experiencing professional bliss owned an online business and loved every minute of it. What did all three have in common? They owned assets, either stocks, real estate, or a business. They traded their time for assets. As Brian Tracy, one of America's best-known motivators, says, "Your greatest asset is your earning ability. Your greatest resource is your time."

Remember!
You are your most important asset.
Your time is your second-most-important asset.

The Man Who Made $15,000 Every Time He Went to the John

I began to really understand the power of assets from a friend of mine who was a "baby" lawyer in a large law firm in the South with about 160 lawyers. He told me the story of his boss, the company's founder.

But before I share the story, let me explain something about how lawyers make money. Lawyers sell their time. They bill in increments of hours for work done on behalf of their clients, anywhere from $200 to over $600 per hour depending on the skill and position of the attorney. Billing for phone time is done in increments of minutes. You can imagine how quickly those fees add up.

Now, these lawyers working for my friend's company were making good money, well over $100,000 or more a year. But they were still RUBs.

Not their boss, though. There was no doubt that this man was a major Rich Idiot. Here's why.

"Robert, you won't believe this," related my friend, who had done the math and now shared the remarkable results with me. "While the top lawyers in my firm are pulling down about $200,000 to $300,000 a year, my boss, the firm's founder, is making about $90,000 an hour, $15,000 every ten minutes! I figured out that when he goes to the bathroom he's making about $17,000 just washing his hands and combing his hair!"

How was that possible?

Simple. This man followed the Rich Idiot secret of acquiring assets. The founder of that law firm owned an asset—in fact, he owned 160 assets, all of them lawyers. The lawyers who worked for him, no matter how big their paychecks, were RUBs—selling their time for dollars.

The founder, on the other hand, took a percentage of the money every single lawyer billed. Whatever he was doing, whether eating breakfast, traveling, or washing his hands in the john, as every one of his 160 lawyers was working, that man was making money. His assets were providing him with benefits.

I got to study that man. And I learned something else from him. Whenever he accumulated a whole bunch of money, he used it to buy even more assets. He bought real estate, shopping centers, stocks and bonds, other businesses, even racehorses. In that way he kept making more and more wealth. It was no wonder he was one of the wealthiest men in the South—a kind of Super Ultimate Rich Idiot.

But this particular story doesn't end there. I used to see him driving around town. Do you want to know what he drove? It was a ten-year-old car. His clothes were simple. He didn't go out much. He was a very humble man. He had some pretty impressive degrees—a master's of psychology, a doctor of divinity, and a doctor of law (despite having dyslexia like me)—but whenever he was introduced to someone he'd always say, "I'm just a simple lawyer from Mississippi trying to make a living. If I can ever do anything personally or professionally for you, do not hesitate to call."

Where Do Rich Idiots Learn to Become Rich Idiots?

Not in school, for the most part. I'm a big believer in education. I support two schools for kids who are just like I was—an idiot in school. Education is great. But the truth is, most Rich Idiots don't learn about assets, liabilities, and all the other secrets of building wealth in a classroom. And I'm talking from personal experience.

After my early adventures in high school, I straightened out and became a RUB. That's right. I pulled up my grades. Followed all the rules. Applied to college. Got in and graduated. I got an MBA and a law degree.

Here's the funny part: If you take the four years I spent in college, and add the four years of graduate school, plus books, transportation, and living expenses, about $250,000 was spent on my education. What had that investment taught me? Not how to create wealth, but how to get a job. And that's what I did. Specifically, my first job right out of school paid me less than $50,000. I traded a $250,000 investment for a return of less than $50,000.

These are RUB rules. This is RUB math.

A Rich Idiot would have followed the Rich Idiot Rule of 72.

I could have taken that $250,000 and put it into some type of an interest-bearing vehicle, calculating its rate of growth by taking the amount of interest—say, 10 percent—and dividing it into 72. A 10 percent rate would mean that my pile of money would double in 7.2 years. Bottom line: Had I respected the power of compound interest and taken the Rich Idiot approach, I might have been sitting on $500,000 seven years after grad school. Instead, I was saddled with two degrees, $250,000 worth of educational debt, and a job that would keep me a RUB until the light finally dawned.

Don't get me wrong; I'm a big believer in education. I just believe people need to educate themselves in how to make and grow money.

The Magic of Compound Interest

Starting Date	Starting Amount	Invested at 10%
Year 1	$20,000	$20,000
Year 2		$24,200
Year 3		$26,620
Year 4		$29,282
Year 5		$32,210
Year 6		$35,431

My Uncle Morris

Uncle Morris was one of the richest men in my family. And for the longest time, while I was a RUB, I never quite understood what he did for a living. For one thing, he was always home. When he wasn't at home in California, he was traveling all over the world, or playing and hanging out with all the kids and cousins. In fact, as a teenager I remember thinking he had a great life: "Does nothing and has lots of money and time." As I became older and more plugged in I discovered that Uncle Morris was one of the first Rich Idiots in our family.

He came to America from Argentina when he was about thirteen or fourteen. His English was so poor that he couldn't get a good job, so he worked in restaurants as a dishwasher. It didn't take him long to figure out that he didn't like washing dishes. So he borrowed some money from family and friends and opened a small restaurant. He worked hard. The restaurant did well. He sold it and bought another one.

Then he started buying low-income property in California.

He quickly discovered that people moving into his houses needed furniture, so he invested in low-income furniture stores.

Uncle Morris never went to school. He never had formal training in how to make money. But his instincts were good and he invested in assets even when he had to borrow to acquire them. And over time all these assets kept making him income while increasing in value.

I remember him always being relaxed and smiling. He supported a lot of family members and was always generous. There is one particular irony that always makes me smile. Even though he was an enormous real-estate investor and owned a large number of properties, he was never able to pass the real-estate agent's exam. Uncle Morris became one of my Rich Idiot role models.

Remember!
Education doesn't guarantee wealth.

RUBs and Rich Idiots: Who Acquires What?
An Amended List

Here's the list again. This time it's complete with the additions of "you" and "your time." Now do your own comparison. Which list most closely resembles your acquisitions?

RUBs	Rich Idiots
Cars	Cash
Furniture	Real estate
Clothes	Stock portfolio
Trips	Businesses
	You
	Your time

Start Buying Assets

Okay, it's time for you to buy your first assets. What's that? I think I hear all those excuses. "Robert, I'm scared. I don't have the time. I'm broke." Stop right now.

- You *can* buy your first stocks, with as little as $10. Online trading allows you to invest as little as $10 for a small fixed fee to set up your account and make stock purchases and sales. There are a number of mutual funds that allow you to buy in for as little as $100. (Go to www.GetRichWithRobert.com for a list of these companies.)

- You *can* buy your first piece of real estate using no money of your own. Many real-estate investors have started real-estate fortunes with not a single penny of their own money—in fact, many didn't even have the ability to borrow, because their credit was either poor or nonexistent. There are many ways to overcome this lack of initial capital. Two of the more popular and suc- cessful strategies are (a) find a partner who either will lend you the money or will allow you to use his credit or (b) find a motivated seller who is willing to allow you to take on the deed to the property with no down payment and favorable terms. These deals and arrangements abound in every real-estate market across the country.

- You *can* start a business using no money of your own. There are many franchise opportunities where the franchisor will finance your start-up business; partnerships with friends who also want to become Rich Idiots can provide some start-up funds; you can simply begin to sell products on the Internet for the cost of a high-speed connection and a Web site; you can join a direct- sales or a quality multilevel marketing company and begin to sell products and sign up members for a revenue and passive- income stream.

You can end up with a very healthy cash asset by investing as little as $1 a day or $250 a week. Just take a look at these two compound-interest tables and see for yourself.

Investment of $1 a Day

Year	Earning interest at 10%
1	$402
5	$2,282
10	$5,903
15	$11,736
20	$21,129
25	$36,256
30	$60,619
60	$1,117,811

Investment of $250 a Week ($13,000 a year)

Year	Earning interest at 10%
1	$13,200
5	$75,018
10	$194,097
15	$385,827
20	$694,639
25	$1,191,984
30	$1,992,964
60	$36,749,959

These and many other ideas and strategies can be found on my Web site, www.GetRichWithRobert.com. Are we done now? There's nothing left to whine or complain about. So let's get started.

I'm about to take you through Robert's Rich Idiot Asset-Acquisition strategy. I'll share all the ways I learned to acquire assets: stocks and bonds, real estate, and businesses. Every single asset I acquired brought me closer to Rich Idiot status, and the minute you start acquiring, you'll also be on your way.

Robert and Wendy's

When I was thirteen, like all Jewish boys I had a bar mitzvah. As is the custom, family and friends brought money in celebration of my new status as a man. My father and I counted up my birthday money. I had a grand total of $1,200.

"According to our traditions, Robert," said my father, "you're a man now and must begin to make your own decisions. You have to decide what to do with this money."

I was a man, but I was still thirteen years old. "I want a new bike," I announced. I couldn't wait to purchase a liability.

"You have to invest it," said my father, pointing me to my first asset and my very first step on the path to Rich Idiot wealth.

"Invest in what?" I answered, trying to figure out how to turn a new bike into an investment my father would approve of.

"Buy some stock" was the response.

"I don't know anything about stocks." The bicycle was disappearing fast.

"Stocks are small pieces of companies you buy and own. Choose a company you like and buy stock in that company."

"I like hamburgers," I said, thinking that if I couldn't get the bike, I could at least get some great burgers. "I like Wendy's hamburgers."

To my surprise, my father took me seriously. He called a stockbroker and got a lot of information about Wendy's. We read it together. He explained to me what to look for in a company. He showed me that Wendy's didn't have a lot of debt on its books at the time. He pointed out that the company was growing. All I knew was that the place had great burgers. So we took my $1,200 to the stockbroker and bought some Wendy's stock. Within two years it had quadrupled—and the surge wasn't from all the burgers I was buying!

Anyway, that's how I began acquiring stocks as a major part of my investment portfolio.

What about you? Is there a particular company whose products and services you use frequently? Is there a particular industry you're interested in? Are your kids playing with toys or games that are growing in popularity? Are your parents and their friends making lifestyle or health purchases from particular companies? All these can be clues to your first stock acquisition.

Robert and Real Estate

You already know how I got started collecting another major asset for my portfolio—real estate. I told you the story of the old man and his wife in that run-down office who owned over one hundred properties free and clear, made an income over $1 million, took six months off every year, and enjoyed themselves while their assets worked to provide them with a true Rich Idiot life.

You know how I followed that man around for over a year, learning everything I could about buying, selling, and managing properties until I finally summoned up the courage to buy a property of my own.

Now let me tell you something you may *not* know. I started buying up a lot of real-estate assets and got pretty good at it. So good, in fact, that I was able to retire at the ripe old age of thirty. The rental income from my properties covered all expenses and provided a good living, allowing me to go out and buy more properties—assets.

Basically I spent my time just hanging out.

Of course, it wasn't long before my buddies, all working in jobs and trading their precious hours for dollars, began to ask how I did it. They wanted to do it, too. They wanted to own "stuff," quit their jobs, and just hang out like me. The questions never let up: "How do you do real estate? How do you buy properties? How do you *not* use your own money? How do you make sure it works? Can I take you to lunch?" I'd say, "Sure, everyone's got to eat." We'd go to lunch and I'd explain the whole thing all over again.

I realized my time was an asset and I was spending too much of it explaining the same things over and over again, even though I wanted all my friends and their friends and their friend's friends to be successful, too.

So I wrote this little twenty-page report and just handed it to anyone who wanted to know how I did it. The next thing I knew, someone suggested it would make a pretty good book. I was retired, with nothing much to do except my real estate, so I handwrote a book (as I mentioned, I have a form of dyslexia that means I can't use a typewriter or keyboard). I self-published it, and to my surprise, the book took off, becoming the first of my many best-selling books on real estate and wealth building.

It also formed the core of a script I've used to build a multimillion-dollar speaking and coaching business.

Now I have even more assets, and the best part is, I can help others, people just like you, to own assets, too, stop trading hours for dollars, and live the life of a Rich Idiot like me.

Robert Gets His First Real Business Asset

As I've said, there are three basic assets: stocks and bonds, real estate, and some form of business. But there's also cash—in the form of savings accounts, CDs, and money market accounts.

I've already told you how I acquired my first stock and real-estate assets. Now I'm about to tell you how I acquired my first business asset.

At the time, I had several properties and many tenants. I believe in ethical landlording, a very radical concept for some landlords. That is, I believe renters should be treated as customers. A tenant of mine suggested that my next book be for renters.

"You're a landlord," he said. "Why not write a book for renters like me? Tell renters how some landlords rip them off. Show them how to protect themselves."

I loved the idea. Here was a real need. Here were people who wanted help. So I wrote a book called *The Renter's Rights Handbook*.

It took off. I was invited to be a guest on TV talk shows. I was interviewed on the radio. Newspapers wrote articles about me and my book.

I was flooded with letters from renters asking for advice. A lot of the advice they wanted and needed was legal advice. I've got a law degree, but I'm not a practicing lawyer. I never have been. I'm a happy lawyer—I have never practiced law. But I wanted to help, so I started to look around for some kind of legal referral service they could use.

Finally, I found what I was looking for, a company called Pre-Paid Legal that provided legal assistance for an affordable flat monthly fee. This was a referral-based marketing company that many RUBs would call a multilevel marketing company or network marketing company. I used the service, thought it was great, and signed up as an associate. The problem was that it was a multilevel marketing company and I was pretty skeptical about these types of firms. So I continued searching for low-cost help for tenants.

Then one evening I was speaking at a meeting attended by about a hundred investors. I happened to mention this Pre-Paid Legal organization I'd found and suddenly sixty-five members of the audience wanted to sign up on the spot (www.GetRichWithRobert.com).

I took another look at the firm, at its reputation, at the way it serviced clients, and decided to try it. I filled out the forms for the sixty-five investors and a week later the company sent me a commission check for $8,000. I thought it was a mistake because, being the Rich Idiot that I am, I'd never bothered to learn about the compensation plan and the payment structure. I just knew that if you signed up people the company would send a check. And it did.

Every subsequent month more and more people at my seminars signed up and got the low-cost legal advice they needed, and I received larger and larger checks. The tenants were happy. I was happy. I now had a business. Tenants got legal advice they needed and investors and businesspeople got good advice, saved money, and got access to great attorneys. I'd created another income stream for myself. I was helping people. I had done some research, filled a need, and now was being rewarded for the activity. And the third asset of my own Rich Idiot plan was in place.

But it didn't end there for me, because, as I learned, success attracts more success. I found myself meeting other successful people. I started hanging out with a more successful crowd. All kinds of new opportunities began to come my way. All of a sudden people were seeking me out. "Robert, you need to meet so-and-so," someone would say. "They've got this great investment opportunity" or "They've got a terrific business idea." I started to meet these exciting, creative people. I began to invest with them and in them.

Now I had cash in the bank, a stock portfolio, real estate, my own business, and shares in the businesses of others. I was asset-rich.

Remember!
Another way to think of RICH:
Residual Income Creates Happiness.

Follow the Asset Path

When I trace my asset path, from that first Wendy's stock purchase because I liked their hamburgers, to my chance meeting with a man who taught me to invest in real estate, to the serendipity of writing the first of my best-selling books (one of which led me to a new and successful business), I'm amazed.

What about *your* path to riches? Mark today as the beginning of your journey. Follow the road where it leads, as I did. Don't be afraid. Trust yourself. Trust the powers that guide you and reveal opportunities. Explore every one. Take action. Have fun. Do good. Enjoy every minute you spend becoming a Rich Idiot.

Remember!
Trust your wealth path and follow where it leads.

Join AA—Asset Allocation

Now that you've got—or are acquiring—all these assets, there are two words that can take you from rich to mega-rich: *asset allocation*. Here's how they work to increase your wealth.

Asset

All Rich Idiots have as their primary goal the accumulation of as many assets as possible. Warren Buffett accumulates shares in companies and reinvests the income from share dividends in more shares. Bill Gates owns a company that throws off massive profits. He takes those profits and reinvests them and the cycle is repeated. Donald Trump owns real estate that generates rental income and appreciation. He takes those monies and buys more real estate.

But if you're looking for role models, I'd encourage you to look beyond such "asset rock stars" as Warren Buffett, Bill Gates, or Donald Trump and check out what's happening in your own town. There you'll find people who've used the same cyclical formula to build lasting wealth.

Your first goal as a beginning Rich Idiot is to acquire your first assets. You don't need a lot of money—in fact, you don't need any money. You can use creative financing techniques, you can borrow, or you can find partners. The key is to begin. Start today.

Allocation

Allocation refers to the way your assets are distributed. It's the number and type of different baskets you put your eggs into—the key word here being "different."

Prudent Rich Idiots never keep all their eggs in one basket. What if you've stored those precious eggs in a stock basket and the basket falls—splat! Now you've got lots of broken eggs. What if you've placed all your eggs in a real-estate basket and the real-estate market takes a dive—more broken eggs. What if every one of your eggs is in your own business basket and you lose a major account—eggshells. When you put all your eggs in one asset basket and that basket breaks, the best you can hope for is an omelet.

Sam's Sad Story

Sam was a distant relative of mine who had made tens of millions of dollars in his recycling business. He had a huge junkyard and collected and recycled industrial junk. Sam was a visionary and way ahead of his time. Today he'd be a hero, and one of the good "green" people.

But disaster struck Sam. The EPA said there was something wrong with the land his business was on—land that had been in his family for over a hundred years. The agency filed a lawsuit against him. He fought back but lost his battle. Sam went from wealthy to broke in a matter of months.

What's the lesson here? If Sam had broadly allocated his assets, he'd be wealthy still. Instead, everything he owned was tied up in his business. When the business he loved disappeared, so did his assets.

It's not disloyal to spread your assets around to protect them. Rather, it's your *obligation* as a Rich Idiot to do just that.

Cash

Cash Is King

You've heard the expression "Cash is king." It's true. Rich Idiots always have a liquid cash basket on their shelf. Cash will give you a sense of security, protect you against sudden asset emergencies, and reduce your stress levels so you'll be able to make better decisions. As a side benefit, it will also create interest income you can roll over and compound. All Rich Idiots want cash flowing into their asset baskets. You can get started today by taking 10 percent of everything you make from now on and creating your first cash basket. Imagine if you had taken 10 percent of everything you earned the past ten years and had it in a cash account today. How would you feel? Start today so in ten years time you'll feel great.

Cash Flow

You've got a zillion dollars coming in every week and half a zillion going out. That's positive cash flow. That's good.

You've got $237.49 coming in every week and $246.08 going out. That's negative cash flow. That's bad.

Sometimes even Rich Idiots, like Sam, get tapped out. The cash stops flowing. There's a cash crunch.

Cash Crunch

You might have a strong stock portfolio, lots of real estate, and several businesses, but all that may not protect you against a cash crunch—or, as the number crunchers say, negative cash flow. Sometimes your cash faucet gets plugged, turned off, or simply dries up. At those times you may need to dip into your cash basket and take out some money.

That's why one of the most important asset allocations is a basket with at least six months' worth of living expenses tucked safely inside. If your living expenses are $5,000 a month (remember to include every single item), you should have at least $30,000 in a safe, liquid checking or savings account. That way, if one of your investments doesn't pan out, or you lose your job, or some other financial disaster strikes, you'll be prepared and will be in a position to hold on to your other assets until you can rebuild again. Personally, I like to have a full twelve months' supply put away for emergencies.

Cash Capital

Finally, one of your baskets should contain cash that's just waiting for a great investment opportunity to arise. You don't want to have to pass it up because you're a little short of ready investment cash.

Remember!
Start putting aside 10 percent of every dollar you earn, today.

Asset Killers

You've got your assets. You've allocated them. Now I'm going to show you how to protect them from the four Ds:

1. Divorce
2. Disability
3. Death
4. "Da government"

Divorce

Here's the good news: The divorce rate is down from about 53 percent of all marriages to about 42 percent. (Love seems to be winning, but I've also heard that part of the reason for the downward trend is that fewer people are getting married.) Here's the bad news: Divorce still wipes out half of all accumulated assets—half of the cash, half of the investments, half of the real-estate holdings, half of the business.

I'm single, but if I get married again I'm going to have a prenuptial agreement. (That's right, I didn't have one the first time around.) Do you know what my prenup is going to say? "If she leaves me, I'm going with her." Because if your spouse leaves, he or she can take half of what you had together.

Here are Robert's Rules for protecting your assets from divorce:

1. *Choose your marriage partner very carefully.* This isn't a relationship book, but I will say that it's important to take your time and make sure you've picked the right partner. You should both have similar value systems and life goals. Your views about money, assets, and wealth should be compatible. Sit down together and discuss your plans for creating and preserving wealth in your marriage *before* you tie the knot.

2. *Sign a prenuptial agreement.* This is very important, especially if you're entering into a second marriage or if there are children from your first marriage. Rich Idiots know that love is love, but money is money and you don't have to share all your wealth with a new spouse and risk the financial future of the rest of your family. Find a good attorney and get that prenup signed.

3. *Be prepared for the worst.* We all enter into marriages hoping they'll last forever, but sometimes things don't work out. If you're developing a lot of investments, make sure you contact an attorney who specializes in creating asset-protection tools. You may be advised to put some of your assets into an irrevocable trust, a limited liability company, a dynasty trust, or some other specialized vessel. Get a good attorney and follow his or her asset-protection advice.

Disability

Disability is a major wealth killer. You may not realize this, but in any calendar year you have a forty times greater chance of becoming disabled than of dying. This isn't meant to frighten or depress you. I'm simply saying that you work hard to create assets; make sure you protect them by protecting yourself.

If you currently work for a company you may have disability insurance, but if you work for yourself you likely haven't taken steps to set this up.

Ask yourself what would happen if you were in an accident or if you became ill and weren't able to work for three months, six months, a year. Would all your bills be paid? Would you have enough money to make your mortgage payments, your car payments, keep your kids in school, buy groceries, and maintain the same lifestyle you have now?

Don't think this doesn't happen to people. As a real-estate investor I see it happen every day. I see people who are suddenly forced to sell their home for 30 percent, 40 percent, even 50 percent below the market price because they became ill for an extended period, blew through their savings, and finally couldn't keep up their payments. These people went from being financially okay to financially ruined. Often these are middle-class, upper-middle-class, and even wealthy families. The reality is, too many Americans are just one or two missed paychecks away from disaster. Are you one of them?

Call a good insurance agent, financial planner, or broker. Make sure you purchase enough disability insurance to protect you.

Death

Another asset killer is death. What many Americans don't know is that if you're not protected by a will or if you don't have the proper trusts set up, your family could lose over half of what you earned over a lifetime. Too many families, even very wealthy ones, have had to liquidate precious assets—land, homes, art collections, family businesses—all because of an unexpected and financially unprotected death that is now subject to a 55 percent estate tax levied by the government. Make sure all your paperwork is in order and inform your family where to find it and what to do. Get with a professional and make sure you have all your paperwork done regarding your health care, your will, trusts, insurances, powers of attorney—so that your financial house is in order. I have examples and referrals for you at www.GetRichWith Robert.com.

"Da Government"

I want you to meet your wealth partner.

"But, Robert, I don't have a partner," you protest.

"Wrong," I say. "You've got a partner, one who possesses a share of every single business, investment, and account you own and who takes anywhere from 20 percent to 50 percent of your assets, depending on where you live and how much you make."

Have you figured out who this partner is yet? That's right. It's the government—federal, state, municipal. And the share your partner takes is in the form of taxes. There are federal income taxes, state income taxes, local income taxes, sales taxes, and property taxes. All these taxes add up and take a big bite out of those eggs in your various baskets.

Now, don't get me wrong: Taxes pay for lots of necessary social benefits—schools, roads, safety, and more. But as a Rich Idiot you're going to make it your goal to legally reduce the amount of taxes you have to pay so you can increase your asset base.

Make sure you're maximizing your tax-reduction and tax-deferral vehicles. Are you using your 401(k) at work? Do you, your spouse, and your children have IRAs? Many self-employed Rich Idiots (like me) have self-directed pension plans and self-directed IRAs, which allow us to determine how and where we invest our retirement funds. If you qualify for one of these programs you can take $44,000 off the top of your income each year, thereby reducing your taxes due. If you're in the 30 percent tax bracket, 30 percent of $44,000 means you could possibly not pay about $13,200 in taxes this year. If you qualify for this you could possibly avoid the payment on these taxes for a very long time! This is a gift from "da government" this year. But many people simply don't know about it.

As a Rich Idiot you'll change your dollar thinking. Every time you get a dollar you won't think, "Wow, I just made another dollar for one of my asset-allocation baskets." No, what you're going to think is: "Wow, I just made another dollar, and after I give my partner his share I'm going to put the rest (anywhere from 50 cents to 80 cents) into my asset-allocation basket." You're going to think in *after*-tax dollars, not *before*-tax dollars.

Remember!
The only dollars that count are *after*-tax dollars.

The Story of Dr. Tommy

Tommy wanted to be a doctor for as long as he could remember. He went to college. He moved on to medical school. He put in hard years getting specialized training. Finally he was ready to open his practice. That's when Dr. Tommy told me over lunch one day, "Robert, I'm so excited. I'm going to make $100,000 a year, and I can't wait to spend it." I hated to break the news to him. "Tommy," I said, "it's time for a reality check. You've got a partner, and by the time you've paid that partner his share, you're going to be left with maybe $60,000 or $65,000 a year." That's when Dr. Tommy's $100,000 bubble burst.

Reducing Your "Partner's" Stake

Here's my advice: Get together with a good accountant and a reliable tax attorney. Work with them to develop and use all the tax write-offs that are legally yours and that you may not be benefiting from right now. Keeping more of your wealth will allow you to live the Rich Idiot life you want and help lots of others live better lives also.

My Last Word About Your Assets

It's never too late to begin. And you don't need any money of your own to get started. In the following chapters you'll see just how easy it can be.

Your Rich Idiot Upside-Down Action Plan

1. Make a list of any assets you may already have.
2. Write down what assets you're going to acquire next.
3. Make an appointment today with a good financial planner, insurance broker, and attorney.

still secret no. 6

Get into Debt

If you think nobody cares if you're alive,
try missing a couple of car payments.
— MERLE TRAVIS

What Do You Mean, Get *into* Debt?

You know by now that when it comes to all things financial, Rich Idiots think and act in a completely upside-down way—that's what makes them Rich Idiots. That same upside-down thinking and behavior also goes for the way Rich Idiots deal with debt. Rich Idiots get *into* debt. Bottom line: If you want to be a Rich Idiot, you'll get into debt, too.

"Hey, Robert, I'm stressed to the max because I'm *in* debt already," you say. "I bought your book because I thought you were going to help me get *out* of debt. I don't get what you're saying here."

Don't get confused or frustrated. What I probably should have said right at the beginning is: Get out of *bad* debt and get into *good* debt.

Remember!
RUBs have "bad debt."
Rich Idiots have "good debt."

Let me explain. There are two kinds of debt: bad debt and good debt. RUBs have tons of bad debt; Rich Idiots have tons of good debt. Bad debt keeps RUBs broke and getting "broker." Good debt makes Rich Idiots rich and helps them get even richer.

You'll catch on really fast because I'm going to share with you some very simple methods Rich Idiots use to lose bad debt and take on good debt. By the time I'm done, you'll be able to put together a Rich Idiot "get out of bad debt and into good debt" plan for yourself.

What's Bad Debt?

Bad debt is the kind of debt you're probably buried under right now. It's the debt you've charged up on your credit cards for everything from yesterday's groceries to the trip you took three years ago and still haven't paid off. It's all those loans with your name on them—money you borrowed for your car, your furnishings, your daughter's wedding, that fishing boat you just had to have. It's all those store credit cards you opened to purchase your fifty-inch flat-screen TV, the baby's stroller along with a month's supply of diapers, and even lawn fertilizer.

All these things fit my definition of bad debt. Why? Because they depreciate—they lose their value and so may be considered liabilities. Remember liabilities, those fun toys and things you consume that eventually consume you?

Let's take a closer look and I'll show you why I call what's on those credit cards, store cards, and loans you've committed to bad debt. Ready?

- Yesterday's groceries—you've already consumed them and they aren't bringing you any money, but now they're on your credit card and you're committed to the debt.
- The trip you took three years ago—you've already taken the trip, stored all your pretty pictures, and hung the lei in the back of the closet. You had a great time but your vacation isn't making

you any money, and you still haven't paid it off. It's a debt that has outlasted the purchase.

- Your loans for your car, your furnishings, your daughter's wedding, and that fishing boat—all those purchases lost up to 50 percent of their value as soon as you took possession of them.

So now you're stuck paying for things that are worth half of what they were worth when you borrowed money to pay for them in the first place. Think about what that means.

The car isn't worth the $38,000 it was when you took out the loan. The minute you drove it off the showroom floor it dropped to $26,600. But the loan is still for the original price. Oops. The same for your boat. And whatever you borrowed for that wonderful new furniture basically became a loan for secondhand stuff the minute the delivery guys took it off the truck. How depressing is that?

Your fifty-inch flat-screen TV, the baby's stroller along with a month's supply of diapers, and the lawn fertilizer you bought last year are all liabilities—no money coming in from them and you've got the debt spread out on a bunch of store credit cards.

Types of Bad Debt
- Bank credit cards with balances that don't get paid in full monthly
- Store credit cards with balances that don't get paid in full monthly
- Bank loans for cars, boats, toys
- Finance-company loans for cars, boats, toys
- Loans for anything that doesn't make money for you

So, What's Good Debt?
Here's one of Robert's quick definitions: Good debt brings in more money than it costs. Let me give you an example. Say you take out a

loan to start a business. If that business brings in more money than the loan is costing you, that's good debt. You've borrowed money to make more money. In other words, good debt is debt that purchases assets. And we've just covered the amazing wealth-building powers of assets.

Interest That's Not So Interesting— in Fact, It's Downright Scary

Let me give you one more example. Let's say you're renting. The way I look at it, you're paying 100 percent interest on your rent money. How can I say that? Because at the end of the month what do you have to show for your $1,000? Nothing. Okay, so you've lived in a place for a month, but it didn't bring you an income. You consumed. Your rent is a consumable. It's done. Gone.

1. Let's run the numbers on your car. Let's say you bought a $20,000 car and the bank is charging you somewhere between 8 percent and 12 percent and your payment is in the neighborhood of $400 a month. The minute you drive that car off the lot it's worth $14,000. So now you're making a $400 payment on a $14,000 depreciating asset (or liability). Every month your car is worth less, but your original loan was based on the price of the car *before* it lost more than a quarter of its value. You're paying on a consumable. That's a no-win situation.

2. The same applies to a trip. You spend $2,000 using a credit card on a vacation, and when you come back you've got nothing to show for it but good times and a memory. But you're still making payments on a credit card. This means you're paying principle and interest on something that's already gone.

3. The same goes for furnishings and other stuff you buy on credit. Say you bought and consumed about $50,000 worth of stuff and put it on your credit cards. Think that's an outrageous number? I bet everybody knows someone who has that much credit card

debt or more. But that stuff isn't worth $50,000 anymore. If you sold it through a garage sale you might get $5,000 for everything. Now let's do the math. If this is you, then your credit cards are charging you about 20 percent interest on that $50,000 of merchandise you've bought. That's about $1,000 a month in payments, or $12,000 over the whole year on stuff that's used and worth only about $5,000. That's over 200 percent in interest.

If you're like most Americans with a RUB mentality, you keep acquiring stuff that's going down, down, down in value from the original price, forcing your debt up, up, up. Pretty soon you run out of money—and oxygen! As Ogden Nash, a famous American humorist, reminds us, "Some debts are fun when you're acquiring them, but none are fun when you set about retiring them."

Remember!
Lose liability debt.
Acquire asset debt.

On the other hand, if you make an investment, even if you use debt to acquire it, now you have an asset. Let's do the math. Say you purchase an asset—in this case, a piece of real estate you buy for $150,000 and on which you pay as much as 10 percent interest. That's about $1,250 a month. But suppose that asset makes you $1,350 a month in rental income after expenses. Now you've got income of $100 a month. Wait, it gets better. That asset appreciates, and when you decide to sell it you may make even more money. You have something that's worth something. You have something that will create income—now and in the future. You have good debt. You're thinking like a Rich Idiot!

Welcome to Debt USA

Right about now you're probably kicking yourself, saying, "What was I thinking? I've got a zillion credit cards, a bunch of loans, and I'm in debt up to my eyeballs." Don't feel too bad. You've got lots of company. A few years ago James Grant, an international business consultant, observed, "The 1980s are to debt what the 1960s were to sex." It hasn't changed in the new millennium. Just take a look at some of these stats:

- Prime Debt Soft reports that the average American household has thirteen payment cards, including credit cards, debit cards, and store cards.
- CNN reports that the average credit card debt per household reached a record $9,312 in 2004. That's an increase of 116 percent over the past ten years.
- *Fortune* magazine reports that the personal savings rate of Americans has dipped into negative territory and was recorded at –0.4 percent of after-tax household income.
- A recent study from ACNielsen revealed that about one in every four Americans doesn't have any spare cash.
- The *Wall Street Journal* reports that 70 percent of Americans live paycheck to paycheck. The shocker is that according to Employee Benefits Trends, this scary statistic fits 34 percent of high earners, those making over $75,000 a year.
- A poll from *Parenting* magazine revealed that 49 percent of Americans could cover less than one month's expenses if they lost their job.
- This credit crisis is worse for young women. A survey of 1,400 women done for the online credit information provider My Equifax found that 10 percent used more than 50 percent of their wages to repay debt each month, compared with 6 percent of men.
- ClearDebt surveyed 5,558 people suffering serious money troubles. Of those, 45 percent were women. One in four of the

women was under twenty-five, and 44 percent of them owed more than their annual take-home pay on credit cards and loans.

- CardTrak reports that making the minimum payments on a $3,000 balance carrying an 18 percent APR will take 431 months (almost thirty-six years) to pay off and cost you $7,511.74 in interest!

Debt Stress

Let's add something else to the bad-debt mix: Any debt that stresses you out is bad debt. Most people in debt focus on interest rates, credit card payments, and dollars and cents. But bad debt carries a second, equally important downside. Bad debt can negatively affect the quality of your perfect life. Debt can add a massive stress burden that can influence your perception of yourself and your success potential and even your health. This type of stress can become all-consuming, filling your thoughts with fears and your spirit with unhappiness.

Writing over a hundred years ago, Ralph Waldo Emerson painted a picture of the stress caused by bad debt: "Debt, grinding debt, whose iron face the widow, the orphan, and the sons of genius fear and hate; debt, which consumes so much time, which so cripples and disheartens a great spirit with cares that seem so base, is a preceptor whose lessons cannot be forgone, and is needed most by those who suffer from it most."

Think of bad debt as a kind of financial bad cholesterol, clogging up your arteries. Think of good debt as a kind of financial good cholesterol, keeping your arteries clear and open.

It happened to me, too, this debt-stress crisis. When my properties were hit by a tornado I had to spend all my cash reserves fixing them up. I was left with absolutely no cash. Every hour, every day all I thought about was how I was going to pay my bills. I had all this debt. I had mortgages. I had credit card debt. I had living expenses, car expenses, and gas expenses. I had very little money coming in. I was consumed by worry about how I was going to juggle the next bill.

That's why I believe that any debt that drains your energy and causes you undue worry is a bad debt and one to be gotten rid of as fast as possible.

Debt and Divorce

Linda M. McCloud, writing for Associated Content, says, "The number one reason people divorce is money." Not everyone agrees with this. But still, most research puts money in the top five reasons for divorce. MSN Money reports, "In a study of married couples from 1980 to 1992, 70% reported some kind of money problems."

Family and Friends Debt

Let's not forget the stress that's added to already precarious family relationships when debt is added to the mix. Many of us have borrowed $5,000 or $10,000 from Mom and Dad, our rich uncle, or a couple of cousins for that next great business deal that never worked out. What happens? Family gatherings are already stressful; add the debt factor and all of a sudden what was a complicated relationship between you and your family becomes supercomplicated. And the issue never goes away. Everyone has a family debt story filled with anger, resentment, and even years of painful silence between the two parties.

This brings to mind a story about two very good friends of mine who lost their friendship over a debt. Let's call them Joe and Ed. Joe loaned Ed $5,000 for a business deal. The business didn't work out. Ed never repaid the debt. Five years went by, and all that time neither spoke to the other. Joe was upset because Ed hadn't paid him back. Ed was furious because he thought Joe was overreacting. More years have since gone by. Both men are now successful. And yet that $5,000 remains unforgiven between them. And the consequences of that are stress, anger, frustration, and the loss of a valuable friendship. In addition, these two men could have gone on to make a lot more money together. That $5,000 turned out to be a very bad debt for both.

Debt Denial

Are you in debt denial? I've worked with a lot of people in foreclosure who were in serious debt. They'd kept borrowing and borrowing, until they were on the brink of losing their homes and everything they had. I can remember banging on the doors of people like this and saying, "Your house is going on the courthouse steps tomorrow at ten A.M. It's going to be auctioned off. You're going to be thrown out. I'm here to help you. Let me buy your house. Let's work out something that's going to be win-win."

You know how these people responded?

"Everything's great."

Of the thousands of people I've talked to who were facing foreclosure, almost 99 percent told me that everything was fine. They all believed something was going to happen to save them. The boss was going to double their paycheck. They would win the lottery. Ed McMahon would show up with a million-dollar check from Publishers Clearing House. They'd win a bundle on the slots, or their $5 lottery ticket would be the big winner. They were in total denial. They needed a debt reality check. What about you? Are you in debt denial? Let's find out. Here are some key warning signs of too much debt. Which ones speak to you?

Warning Signs of Too Much Debt

1. You don't have any savings.
2. You make only the minimum payments on your credit cards.
3. Your cards are precariously close to their maximum limit.
4. You use one credit card to pay off another.

5. You have more than three credit cards with balances that never get paid off.

Let's Take Your Financial Temperature

This is scary for many people, but believe me, this is a critical step on the Rich Idiot pathway. Get out a piece of paper and write down these numbers:

Monthly Payments

Your mortgage payment (including taxes and insurance) or your monthly rent payment	$_____
Your home-equity line of credit or loan payment	$_____
Your car payment	$_____
Your credit card payments	$_____
Other monthly loan amounts	$_____
Any other monthly debts	$_____
TOTAL	$_____

Monthly Income

Take-home salary	$_____
Any other income	$_____
TOTAL	$_____

RESULTS: If your monthly debts are higher than your monthly income, you are in the *red* zone and must begin a bad-debt-reduction program immediately. Ready?

Let's Get You Out of Your Bad Debt

But before we do, I want to say a word about *really* bad debt. There's bad debt, and then there's really bad debt. And don't panic if this is you. We've all done it. We've all been there. Even me. Even most, if not all, Rich Idiots. Really bad debt is the money you borrow to pay off your basic bad debt. When I was in trouble and faced tons of bad debt and couldn't make my payments, the first thing I did was run around trying to borrow even more money. I borrowed more against my properties, against my business, against my credit cards. That's a no-win scenario. That's like an alcoholic saying, "Gee, I want to stop drinking so I'm going to go out and get myself another big bottle of booze." Or like a drug addict saying, "I'm on cocaine and I can't get off it, so I'm going to get myself another big fix tonight and that'll help me shake my habit tomorrow." Duh. Here is a huge Robert Rule: *Debt will not cure debt.*

But there are ways to get you out of debt. Let's get started right now.

Get Real

First of all, I've got some really good news. In the United States not paying your debts is no longer a crime except in specific circumstances. In England many years ago such behavior could land you in debtors' prison. America doesn't have debtors' prisons, so while you may be in financial trouble, ask yourself, "What's the worst that could happen?" I know that fear keeps a lot of you from taking any action. The way I reduce my fear is to look at the worst possible scenario. What if all my real-estate holdings went to zero? What would happen to me? I'd still eat. I'd still have a place to live. I'd still have my ability to make money.

The first thing you need to do is lose your fear. You *can* get out of debt. There are lots of ways you can do it. Don't let fear make your bad-debt situation even worse.

Have Fun

You think I'm kidding. I can hear you now: "Robert, I'm in such trouble and you're telling me one of the ways to get out of trouble is to have fun? What's wrong with you?"

Nothing is wrong with me. Your "get out of bad debt" plan must have as its first objective "have fun." Life is a precious gift. Time is the most valuable thing you have—more valuable than all the wealth and riches you can acquire. Every moment you spend worrying is a moment you've destroyed and can't get back. Your debt can and will be managed. Now put a smile on your face. Give someone you love a hug. Congratulate yourself. Feel the relief. Let the joy come in. You're about to get advice on a whole bunch of ways to get out of bad debt and improve your life. Are we having fun yet?

Make a Plan

You've just finished taking your financial temperature. Now take another piece of paper and write down all the debt you have and where it is. Make a list of every loan and the outstanding amount. Make a list of every credit card that has a balance on it, and the amount of the balance. Now go back and read your credit card statements. You're looking for the interest amount you're being charged on a monthly basis. Write down the interest rate beside each card. Don't worry if the interest rates are different. You'll find that they can vary from 12 to 28 percent. Take your time. This plan is going to tell you not only where you stand today, but also how quickly you can reduce all those numbers.

Make a Promise: Follow the Five Credit Card Commandments

1. Cut up all your credit cards except one.
2. Resist all attempts to get you to sign up for new credit cards.

3. Never charge food, clothing, or entertainment on a credit card.

4. Pay more than the minimum balance each month until the obligation is paid off.

5. Pay credit cards on time to avoid late charges and interest increases.

Do the Trash-Can Demo

It's important to have a strong visual picture of just how much credit cards are costing you. Whenever I do this demo with anyone, they never forget it. Go ahead now and try it for yourself.

Take out whatever money you have in your wallet or purse. Let's say, for example, it's $100. Take one-fifth, or $20, and throw it in the garbage can. That amount roughly represents the average interest payment you're making on any unpaid credit card balance. You're not done yet. Now take another 30 percent of what was in your wallet and throw that into the garbage can, too. That roughly represents the percentage of what you'll pay in taxes. In other words, half of what you think is your money isn't. Half is going into the trash. Perform this demonstration in front of your whole family. You'll see that garbage can every time you take out a credit card to pay for something, and it'll be a great incentive to reduce the card's usage.

Start Paying Off Credit Card Debt

There are two schools of thought about how to pay off credit card debt. One school recommends paying off the card with the highest interest rate, because that's the card that's costing you the most money.

The second school advocates what I call the "snowball" approach. Here's how it works: Say you have five credit cards, all with balances on them. The first has a balance of $10,000, the second $6,000, the third $4,000, the fourth $2,000, and the fifth $1,500. You pay off the $1,500 balance first. Then you take the money you were using to pay off that balance and apply it, along with the minimum payment, to the card with the next-biggest balance—in this case, the one on which you owe the $2,000. In that way you pay that fourth card's balance off quickly. You do the same with the third card and then the second. Using this method, you feel like you're accomplishing something every month—and, indeed, you are.

Make a Call

This is a Rich Idiot strategy. Learn this skill and you'll be able to incorporate it into all your future financial dealings. I realize that for many of you this is going to be difficult, but I assure you that you can make a lot of money by just picking up the phone and asking for a reduction in either the total amount of debt you owe or the amount of interest you're being charged or both.

On your loan or credit card paperwork there should be, in each case, a customer service number. When you get a human being on the line, ask to speak to someone who has the ability to authorize a reduction in your loan payments or your interest rate. Hang firm. Stay on the line until you get someone who can really make a decision.

Here's what you say: "I'd like your company to reduce the amount of this debt so I can pay it off. I would also like you to reduce the interest rate and the monthly payments to help me." Chances are good that companies will work with you to reduce either the debt or your interest rate or your monthly payments.

When you're talking to a credit card company, you should also let the agent know that you have researched other credit card companies and their interest rates, and you've found that you can do better somewhere else. Often your existing credit card company will reduce its interest rate to match that of a competitor.

What's the upside of this strategy? You may have less bad debt to pay off, at a more favorable rate. What's the downside? Even if the agent says no, you're no worse off than you were before you picked up the phone.

Go for it.

Get a Credit Counselor

Remember, Rich Idiots use O.P. (Other People) Power. So think about adding a credit counselor to your Rich Idiot Dream Team. It doesn't matter that you're in debt. This one step alone will empower you, give you vital information, and add a power player who has the expertise to help you reach not only your debt-reduction goals but also your wealth goals. This is also a good strategy for reducing the stress that results from too much bad debt. All of a sudden you have an expert negotiating your debt repayment in a manner that will work in your favor. You've secured relief from creditors' phone calls and dunning letters. You've created a solid plan and obtained the help to implement it. This is Rich Idiot thinking and acting all the way!

Accumulate Extra Debt-Repayment Money

Sell Your Stuff

Go through your entire house, including the basement, garage, and attic, and your storage unit, if you have one, and pull out anything that's saleable. Have a huge garage or lawn sale and trade your stuff for extra cash. Anything left over can be sold on eBay, through a consignment shop, or by placing a small ad in your local paper.

Sell Other People's Stuff

Visit your family, friends, and neighbors and ask if they have stuff you can haul away and sell for them. Don't be too proud to explain that this is part of your effort to raise extra money to get out of debt. Offer to do the work and split the proceeds fifty-fifty. Chances are, your family and friends will be so relieved to see you working toward a positive solution, while getting rid of their own unwanted stuff, that they'll let you keep the whole amount you raise.

Downsize

This is what I did. And I consider it one of my best decisions ever. Like everybody else, I had a huge overhead. I had an office, a big house, lots of cars, lots of expensive toys. It was fun, but it was also costly. I had to buy all that stuff, maintain it, store it, insure it, and move it. I decided it just wasn't necessary. I got rid of my huge house, the office, most of the toys. The result? Cash to pay off bad debt. Cash to invest in good, asset-based debt.

Organize a Fund-raiser

This is one of the most ingenious "get out of bad debt" strategies I've ever heard of, and the idea was inadvertently hatched in one of my own seminars.

A young lady named Amanda came to one of my seminars and she was in debt—big-time. She listened to me talking about using your creative powers to vanquish debt and the next day at our follow-up session raised her hand to speak. "Robert," she said, "I just want to tell you that when I sat down in your seminar yesterday morning I was $8,000 in debt. This morning my debt is down to $4,000. I want to thank you for all your help."

Well, I was really surprised and intrigued. This was one of the most astonishing "get out of bad debt" successes I'd ever heard of. "Would you like to share with the rest of us how you did it?" I asked. She went on to explain that she simply held her own personal fundraiser. She called her family and friends and asked them to "pledge" funds to help her reduce her debt. Remarkably, no one turned her down! And from her point of view, the best part of the campaign was not only debt reduction, but these were pledges, not loans, so there was no repayment on her part.

Get Yourself a "Get Out of Bad Debt" Job

Another effective strategy is to take a part-time job and direct the extra earnings toward paying off your bad debt faster. If you look around you may be able to find flexible jobs, such as babysitting or waiting on tables (tips can help).

Get a Consolidation Loan

Sometimes it makes fiscal sense to take a consolidation loan, which is typically a home-equity line at a relatively low rate of interest, and use those funds to pay off higher-interest credit cards. Another advantage of a consolidation loan is that this type of financing is generally available over a longer period of time, thus lowering your minimum monthly payment. While I don't advocate getting into more debt, this is one exception, providing you use the equity line to pay off your credit cards, then cut them up.

The "B" Word

Declaring bankruptcy can help you wipe out some or most of your debt and offer you a chance to start again. However, it carries heavy penalties. Your credit will be negatively affected, your self-image may be damaged, and you may encounter hostility from creditors who see the strategy as unethical. In any event, this debt-reducing strategy should be undertaken only after consultation with an attorney who specializes in this area.

Rich Idiots and Good Debt

Let's do a quick recap regarding good debt and why Rich Idiots use it to get even richer. Good debt is debt you assume that brings in more money than it costs. Good debt could be a loan you take out to start a business. If that business brings in more money than the loan is costing, that's definitely good debt. You've borrowed money to make more money. In other words, good debt is debt that purchases assets. It could be a loan you take out to purchase real estate, or to invest in stocks, bonds, or mutual funds, or it could be borrowed money you put into savings at a higher rate than the interest rate at which you borrowed it.

What's the Optimum Length of Time to Carry Good Debt?

This is a great question, and one I'm asked all the time. How long you should commit to carrying good debt depends on your personality and your tolerance for debt stress.

If you make decisions based more on economics than emotion, you'll take out a good-debt loan for as long as possible. This is how I arrange for my good debt. I borrow as much money as I can for as long as they'll loan it to me: twenty years, thirty years, one hundred years— however long I can stretch it. This is a Rich Idiot strategy. Make sure that your returns are much more than the cost of the debt.

If you make decisions based more on emotion than economics and are the type who craves security and worries about long-term financial obligations, you'll want to borrow money for a shorter term. Get over it. This mentality runs counter to the Rich Idiot mind-set.

Rich Idiot Debt Thinking

Let's take a peek into the inner workings of the Rich Idiot moneymaking machine. There's a little math coming, but it's fun and the numbers will surprise you.

Example 1

Rich Idiots think of debt as a tool. Let's say you plunk down $10,000 cash for a stock, a piece of real estate, or any investment. And let's also say that every year, that $10,000 brings you a return of $1,000. You've just made a 10 percent return on your investment. Not too shabby. But it's not really Rich Idiot thinking. Before you pat yourself on the back, take a look at this.

Example 2

Let's say you put down $100 and then go to the bank and borrow $9,900 at a nice interest rate. You've checked and double-checked your numbers and find that your investment still throws off $1,000 a year. For the sake of this example, let's say your loan costs you $800 a year. The difference between the $1,000 you're making and the $800 you have to pay back every year is $200. So now what's the bottom line? You've just made $200 on a $100 investment (remember, $100 was what you put down—the bank put down the rest). Now your return on your investment is 200 percent. And there's a bonus: If the investment is one that allows you a tax write-off, you get to make even more money. This is called leveraging. It's how Rich Idiots turn what you might call bad debts (loans) into good debts (leverage). But there's a caveat. You must really do your research and talk to other Rich Idiots before you make this kind of investment. Wait till you get the green light.

Warning!
Rich Idiots only borrow money they definitely
know that they can pay back.

Rich Idiots and Credit Cards

Rich Idiots love credit cards. And they use them to make money and get perks. Here's how it works:

Generally speaking, some Rich Idiots use only two credit cards. One is for business expenses, the other for personal. Rich Idiots run up huge balances on their cards—$25,000 and up every month—but they also pay off those balances in full every month. Rich Idiots don't let credit card balances revolve. This strategy gives them free use of OPM (Other People's Money) for a full month while their money is sitting in an investment making even more money, at the rate of 8, 10, or 18 percent.

The other big reason Rich Idiots make frequent use of their cards is that most credit cards offer points. The more points, the more free goodies. I travel a lot, so I've got hundreds of thousands of points saved up, which I use for free travel, upgrades, products, hotels, and more. I also give away my points to people who need a place to stay or to charities, which use them to help the less fortunate.

Rich Idiots and the Ubiquitous Credit Score

Some Rich Idiots don't care about their credit scores. Of course, a good credit score is nice, but the reality is, Rich Idiots typically use other people's credit and other people's money, so the credit score doesn't really factor in. Although I have purchased lots of properties, I have not used my credit score to borrow money. Once you learn how to use other people's money and credit, you will probably stop using your own, too.

Rethinking the Zero

Now that you know the difference between bad debt and good debt, let's end this chapter with a stretching exercise. You've probably been thinking that you need to reduce the number of "debt zeros" in your life. That's true only if they're zeros attached to bad debt. To become a true Rich Idiot you should practice thinking about *adding* zeros to your debt—your good debt.

Here's a story that will show you how thinking past your "zeros barrier," or comfort zone, can accelerate your wealth dramatically.

A friend of mine owned a small condo for which she'd paid $119,000. It was lovely and she was very proud to be a home owner. Two years after she purchased the property, her financial adviser suggested that she purchase a larger, more expensive home. Together they worked out the dollar amount of the house she could own. She was shocked to learn that she could purchase a $750,000 home. Her comfort zone had been in the $200,000 range. But she took the plunge, purchased the new home, and four years later sold it for $1,250,000! By adding some zeros to her debt tolerance she made $500,000.

The lesson? Rich Idiots think in bigger numbers. Try it.

Your Rich Idiot Upside-Down Action Plan

1. Make a list of all your assets.
2. Make a list of all your liabilities.
3. Make a plan to pay off your bad debt.
4. Make a plan to acquire good debt.
5. Get my "Get Ready to Get Rich Planner" at www.GetRichWithRobert.com.

still secret no. 6

Three Deals and You're Done

*It is a comfortable feeling to know that you stand on your own ground.
Land is about the only thing that can't fly away.*
— ANTHONY TROLLOPE

The Asset Known as Real Estate

There's one thing you need to become a Rich Idiot, and that's assets. Now, as you already know, there are three types of assets: real estate, stocks, and your own business. Acquiring any one will help make you a Rich Idiot. Acquiring all three can make you not only a Super-Rich Idiot, but a super-savvy Rich Idiot.

Why all three? Because as you've already learned, you need to put your assets into different baskets to keep them safe. That way, if one of your asset baskets breaks and you lose the contents, you've still got lots of lovely baskets filled with lots of lovely assets.

Let's look at how neatly real estate fits the asset definition. You'll remember that all true assets share these three characteristics.

1. They have value.

Real estate has value. It has value with respect to both the building and the land.

2. You own or control them.

If you are on the deed or have a lease-option contract, you control the property.

3. They provide you with future benefit (a.k.a. money).

Real estate provides you with future benefits by way of tax depreciation, capital gains, rental income, and appreciation wealth. You can also use leverage to buy real estate without using your own money.

You can see that real estate is a powerful asset. It's the one that got me started on my own road to riches, and if this Rich Idiot could do it, believe me, so can you. Let's begin.

Rich Idiots *Love* Real Estate

Whether it's my friend Donald Trump saying, "It's tangible, it's solid, it's beautiful. It's artistic, from my standpoint, and I just love real estate," or Suze Orman announcing, "Owning a home is a keystone of wealth [that provides] both financial affluence and emotional security," there's no doubt that real estate is the favored asset of many wealth experts.

You, too, can become a Rich Idiot, with only three pieces of real estate. That's right: Just by purchasing three properties—your own home and two investment properties—over three years and holding them, you can cash out in twenty years with almost $4 million or in thirty years with over $7 million. And that's with just the most simple, conservative real-estate strategy. If you add in more deals and employ more creative wealth-generating investment strategies, you can increase your return and shorten the length of time it takes you to become a Rich Real-Estate Idiot.

Remember!
Rich Idiots get the money first, then the house.
RUBs look for the house first and then can't get the money.

First, I'm going to show you the dramatic numbers you can achieve with just three simple deals. Then I'm going to show you how to get richer faster with some creative acquisition strategies and my own Robert's Real-Estate Rules for investors.

As you know, real estate, like any investment, can go up, can go down, or can stay the same. Appreciation, interest, and expense rate can vary. I normally teach people to buy below market values and do research so they are comfortable. These figures below are just examples to illustrate how the process can work.

Deal 1 — Own Your Own Home

Price you paid	$300,000
Term of mortgage	20 years
Interest rate	7%
Appreciation/year	6%

Time Frame	Value of Property	Amount of Mortgage Remaining
5 years	$404,655	$257,953
10 years	$545,819	$180,000
20 years	$993,061	$0
30 years	$1,806,773	$0

Deal 2 — Your First Income Property

Price you paid	$400,000
Term of mortgage	20 years
Interest rate	7%
Appreciation/year	6%

Time Frame	Value of Property	Amount of Mortgage Remaining
5 years	$539,540	$343,927
10 years	$727,759	$240,976
20 years	$1,324,082	$0
30 years	$2,409,030	$0

Deal 3	Your Second Income Property
Price you paid	$500,000
Term of mortgage	20 years
Interest rate	7%
Appreciation/year	6%

Time Frame	Value of Property	Amount of Mortgage Remaining
5 years	$674,425	$429,922
10 years	$909,698	$331,939
20 years	$1,655,102	$0
30 years	$3,011,288	$0

Three Deals and You're Done—Rich Idiot, Check Out These Numbers

Deal	20 years	30 years
1	$993,061	$1,806,773
2	$1,324,082	$2,409,030
3	$1,655,102	$3,011,288
TOTAL	$3,972,245	$7,227,091

Congratulations! You're a millionaire *and* a Rich Idiot! Let me just add a word about the numbers I used in these three examples. I chose them to illustrate my point, that all it takes is three deals. You can substitute other numbers. For example, if your home cost $150,000, your second deal cost $175,000, and your third deal cost $290,000, your result will be different. Similarly, if your home cost $450,000, your second deal came in at $280,000, and your third deal closed at $420,000, those results will also be different. For a quick and simple way to figure out exactly what your own bottom line will be, go to my Web site, www.GetRichWithRobert.com, and use the amortization and appreciation tables provided.

Three Deals Through a Money Microscope

Let's take a closer look at these three deals and see just how they work.

Deal 1: Your Own Home

If you already own your own home, pat yourself on the back. You have acquired your first real-estate asset. You've done one deal. You've learned how to negotiate and place an offer. You've applied for and been granted a mortgage. You've successfully dealt with contracts, purchase agreements, and closing documents. You've closed on your first property. You're one-third of the way to becoming a Rich Idiot. And now you're eligible for tax benefits such as tax-free capital gains (as much as $250,000 if you're single and $500,000 if you're a couple) on the appreciation of your property. You can sit back for a while and take a break.

Remember!
Practically every lender in America has a program
for first-time home buyers.

If you're renting from someone else, the first thing you have to do is stop and purchase your own home. Rich Idiots don't rent. Rich Idiots own. Rent, as you already know, is not an asset. It's a liability. At the end of the lease year all you have is twelve canceled checks. True, you've had a roof over your head, but it's someone else's roof. They own the asset—you don't. They get the tax benefit of depreciation—you don't. They get the tax benefit of appreciation—you don't. They get the tax write-offs—you don't. They get the equity increase every year as the value of the property goes up—you don't. They get all this and they're not even paying for it—you are! Duh. Every month you send in a rent check is a month you're getting further and further away from becoming a Rich Idiot, while your landlord is getting closer and closer. It's time to turn this around. Of course there are reasons to rent—if you are planning to move in less than a year.

Okay, here it comes. I can hear all the protests from the renters right now: "But, Robert, I've got no money for a down payment." Or "Robert, I've got lousy credit." Or "Robert, I don't have a job—how can I make my payments?" Poor you. As long as you're in the middle of your own pity party, I can't help you. The minute you decide to become a home owner is the minute you take your first step toward real money. So get over all the excuses and understand this: There are dozens of ways to get your first home without using a dime of your own cash and with the worst credit in the world. Check out the resources on my Web site, www.GetRichWithRobert.com.

By the way, if you do get your first home using OPM (Other People's Money), congratulate yourself, because you've just learned one of the most important lessons in creating wealth. By using Other People's Money you don't risk any of your own (forget that you may not have any to risk), and when you sell or refinance your home purchased with Other People's Money, your rate of return is infinite. Confused? Don't be. It's simple.

As I've said, Rich Idiots think of debt as a tool. Let's say you plunk down $100,000 cash for your piece of real estate. And every year, that $100,000 appreciates 10 percent, or $10,000. You've just made a 10 percent return on your investment.

Now take a look at that same real-estate investment if you purchased it entirely with Other People's Money.

Let's say you put up zero dollars of your own and a private lender or a partner put up the entire amount or let you use their credit. Let's also say the mortgage rate you got was 7 percent. Keeping it really simple (you can use more exact tables), you can see that $100,000 is costing you $7,000 a year. But your property could be going up in value by 10 percent a year, or $10,000. What's your profit? It's $3,000 a year. What's your return on investment? Infinity. You didn't use a penny of your own money, so any revenue generated represents the best rate of return possible!

And as an added bonus for thinking like a Rich Idiot, you get all the tax benefits due a home owner. As you'll recall, this is called leveraging—it's how Rich Idiots acquire assets.

By the way, don't think that you can purchase only trash property this way. That's not true. You can purchase any type of property with none of your own capital, from small starter homes right up to million-dollar luxury properties—and beyond.

So don't worry if you don't possess any money for your first real-estate deal—be happy. Go out and get your first deal done today.

Deal 2: Your First Income Property

Now that you have Deal 1 under your belt, you've only got two more to go. Deal 2 is going to be your first income or rental-property asset. It can be a single-family home or a small duplex. You should purchase this property within two years of closing on your first deal.

The first thing I want you to do is relax and stop thinking. I know what's in your head. I can practically hear the RUB script from here. The noise is deafening. "Robert, I don't really need another house. I'm comfortable with just this one. It's manageable. I don't have time to look for another deal. I don't want the hassles of becoming a landlord. I don't want to deal with 'my toilet's flooded' calls in the middle of the night. I don't want to worry about finding a good tenant. I don't want to lose sleep over tenants who skip without paying their rent . . . blah, blah, blah."

Listen up. Every single one of those thoughts is RUB-think.

You're thinking you've got to do all this alone, right? Calm down and just remember your first deal. You had a real-estate agent find it for you. You had a banker arrange the financing. You had a lawyer go over the contracts. You had a title company complete the closing. You weren't alone when you did your first deal. Guess what? You won't be alone in your second deal, either. You can use a real-estate agent to help you find a great investment property. Your bank will arrange for your financing. Your lawyer will review the contracts, and your closing company will close. Your original Dream Team is still in place and working for you. The only additions you'll need to make to that Dream Team with the acquisition of your second real-estate asset are a good contractor or handyman to undertake any repairs and a part-time property manager to handle rentals and tenants. Just ask the members of your local real-estate investment club or your real-estate agent for referrals. If you're worried about how much these folks will cost, here are some guidelines. Generally these fees are negotiable. Property management ranges from 8 to 10 percent; a handyman or someone who collects the rent usually charges a basic hourly rate. Many investors find good help in their tenants. Often a tenant will undertake to do basic maintenance, repair, and rent collection in exchange for a reduction in his or her own rent.

Stop worrying right now and go back and reread Chapter 5, about O.P. Power.

Let's concentrate instead on the numbers. How much should you pay for your second deal? There is a very simple formula. The cost of your acquisition should be equal to or less than (I prefer less than) the income. Let's flip that around and look at it the other way. Your rental income should cover the cost of your property. The standard costs are the mortgage payment, insurance, and taxes. You also need to factor in approximately 8 to 10 percent for a property manager, 10 percent for vacancy, in case you don't rent your property as quickly as you would like, and to allow you a little time between tenants to go in and paint and make any necessary repairs and improvements, and about 15 percent for repairs depending on the age and condition of the property. These figures can work monthly or annually. As a Rich Idiot I like to keep things real simple—so I calculate everything monthly. Guidelines are not to have negative cash flow.

Let's put some sample numbers behind this so you can see exactly what I mean.

Deal 2

Purchase price	$150,000
Mortgage rate	7%
Mortgage payment	$1,620 per month
Insurance	$50 per month
Taxes	$200 per month
Vacancy rate	10%
Property manager	8–10 percent
Repairs	15%
TOTAL COSTS	$2,106 per month

Your total costs are $2,106 per month. That means you need to find a tenant who will pay you at least $2,106 per month. If your $150,000 purchase is a duplex, each unit should rent for at least $1,053 per month. Remember. Keep it simple. All real estate is, is what comes in every month and what goes out. So make sure you double- and triple-check all the income and all the expenses before you invest.

Financing your first investment property generally follows the same rules as those for financing your first property, your own home. Try to use other people's money as much as possible, and check your numbers to make sure you haven't made any mistakes in figuring the cash going out. Also, make sure that the rental income you need is realistic for your area. This can be determined with a quick phone call to a rental company or a simple glance at your local paper. Once you've checked your numbers, go out and buy Deal 2, your first investment property.

Deal 3: Your Second and Final Income Property (but You Don't Have to Stop at Three)

Here's your third and final real-estate-asset acquisition. It should be a larger rental unit—a fourplex, sixplex, or small apartment building. You should purchase it within three years of purchasing your first property.

I'm hearing the panic again. But this is simply more of the same stuff you've already done twice, successfully.

Everything is the same. The only difference may be in your financing. When you look for mortgage money for properties that contain more than four living units, you fall into the commercial-lending category. In fact, this category can be better, because lenders now change their focus. They stop scrutinizing you and your credit worthiness and focus on the property and its real value. From a risk point of view, this is wonderful news for you. When you get approval for a mortgage against a larger property, you can be sure that the lender has checked and double-checked the value, the appreciation, the potential income, and the resale worth of that property. And the more confident the lender is in the deal, the less risk to you.

Let's run some numbers for Deal 3 and see exactly how they work. Remember, the numbers I'm using are sample numbers only—so make sure, when you find a property you like, that you follow the same kind of process.

Deal 3

Purchase price	$300,000
Mortgage rate	7%
Mortgage payment	$2,325 per month
Insurance	$75 per month
Taxes	$300 per month

Vacancy rate	10%
Property manager	8–10%
Repairs	15%
TOTAL COSTS	$3,510 per month

Your total costs are $3,510 per month. That means you need to find people who together will pay you at least $3,510 per month. If you have six tenants, each unit should rent for $585 per month or more.

You're Done!

That's it. You've just done your three deals. That's all you have to do to become a Rich Idiot. Of course, if you're like most Rich Idiots, once you get started you're going to want to continue. Why stop at three real-estate assets? Why not go to four, five, ten, a hundred, or more? No reason. Because with each deal you do, you'll learn more, you'll become more confident, and you'll increase your wealth and reach your perfect Rich Idiot life much sooner.

Pyramid of Real-Estate Assets

There's a wide variety of properties you can purchase. For discussion purposes I like to arrange them in a pyramid shape.

Single-Family Houses

This is the largest category and forms the base of my pyramid. These are generally two- or three-bedroom homes in a moderate price range. Sometimes they're referred to as cookie-cutter homes.

The advantages of these are that they're relatively easy to buy and sell in any kind of market and there's always a rental market with lots of available tenants. Even in a down market this classification of single-family homes seems to sell well and even enjoys some appreciation if located in the right area.

The primary disadvantage is that they may need more management. For example, you may find yourself with five houses with five tenants in five different and geographically scattered neighborhoods.

Duplexes, Triplexes, and Fourplexes

On the second level of our real-estate-assets pyramid are duplexes, triplexes, and fourplexes—all classed as rental properties.

The advantages are that mortgage lenders consider properties up to and including fourplexes "residential" and therefore apply far less stringent lending requirements—in fact, in many instances you can get 100 percent financing for these. The other advantage of owning them is that they provide some economies of scale, with two, three, or four renters in the same building.

The disadvantages reveal themselves when you want to sell one. The only buyers will be other investors, so now your market is a little smaller.

Small to Medium Apartment Buildings

The third level of the pyramid is composed of small- to medium-sized apartment buildings. These can contain as few as ten units or as many as 150.

The advantages are more cash flow because of a wider tenant base, the potential for greater economies of scale, and even the addition of a full-time property or resident manager. Lenders also help reduce your investment risk because they scrutinize the property for its income potential before they lend you funds. And, finally, lenders may require as little as 20 percent down on a property that provides a comfortable cash flow.

One disadvantage is that you'll have to come up with a larger down payment—as much as 20 percent to get good financing. Also, you'll need a bigger cash cushion to allow for vacancies. And, again, should you decide to sell, your only buyers will come from a smaller pool of more sophisticated investors.

Commercial Property

At the very top of the real-estate pyramid sits commercial property. This includes large apartment complexes, office buildings, strip malls, and storage facilities.

A big advantage of owning these real-estate assets is that you'll be able to negotiate leases whereby the tenants (particularly corporate tenants) are responsible for much of the management and property repairs. Also, the property generally provides a good cash flow and can sustain the cost of full-time management.

The disadvantages are that, once again, your only buyer is likely to be another investor and should you lose a prime tenant—one commanding several floors of a corporate office building or an anchor tenant in a strip mall—the property may remain vacant longer. This creates a need for a larger cash cushion to carry you through several lean months or even years.

What's a Good Deal?

For a Rich Idiot there aren't any distinctions between types of real-estate investments. Whether you concentrate on single-family homes, apartment buildings, or commercial property, it always comes down to the numbers. It's all about the numbers. If the numbers work, you've got a good deal. If the numbers don't work, you don't. A good deal means finding a motivated seller who is willing to let you have the property at 20 to 50 percent below today's market value. Those deals are out there, but most people are not willing to go out and look for them.

Robert's Rules of Rich Idiot Real Estate

Here are some very fast, simple rules to follow as you begin to acquire your own real-estate assets. These rules are the result of my own years of experience as a real-estate investor and the combined experience of the thousands of people just like you who became Rich Idiots follow-ing these rules.

Robert's Rule No. 1: Set a Real-Estate Investment Goal

There are three types of real-estate investment goals: short-, medium-, and long-term. Let's take a quick look to determine which suits you best.

Short-Term Goal: I want to get in and out of a property fast. I need cash in the next thirty, sixty, or ninety days. I want to pay off some bills. I want to take a trip. I want or need quick cash. I need money to invest in something else.

Short-Term Strategy: Wholesale a property: Put a good deal under con-tract, then sell it to another investor and make some money on the transaction.

Medium-Term Goal: My time frame for buying and selling a property is three to eighteen months.

Medium-Term Strategy: You're going to fix up and hold the property or even rent it out for a short period of time. You're in a strong apprecia-tion market and/or you buy the property at a big discount and can make money when you sell or refinance at the end of a year.

Long-Term Goal: You purchased a property that you're going to keep for three to five years or longer.

Long-Term Strategy: This is pretty much always your own home or a rental property. You're planning to hold it and wait until the appre-ciation mounts up, tenants pay the cost of your investment, or both. At the end of your long term you'll decide whether to sell or refinance.

What's the right goal and strategy for you? I recommend the sim-ple "Three Deals and You're Done" scenario, covered earlier in this chapter. You purchase three properties over a period of one to three years, hold them, and then either sell or refinance. That's your best Rich Idiot real-estate plan.

Robert's Rule No. 2: Buy from Motivated Sellers

In real-estate circles, it's said that you make your money not when you sell a property but when you buy it. The better the deal you can cut at the time of purchase, the greater your profits and your spread between expenses and rental income, and the greater your equity. One of the best ways to ensure that you purchase your properties at Rich Idiot prices is to purchase them from motivated sellers.

Now, when I say "motivated sellers," I want to be very, very clear. I'm not talking about taking unfair or unethical advantage of people. I'm talking about buying from folks who have to sell because of divorce, an unexpected move, even a financial setback, but structuring the deal so that both parties win.

A student of mine—let's call him Jim—told this great story about a motivated seller at one of my seminars, and I'd like to share it with you.

Jim is a twenty-one-year-old real-estate investor and likes to buy, fix up, and resell houses. One day he was working on a property when he took a wrong turn and ended up on a nearby street. He noticed a large property that was boarded up. He did a little investigating, and when he went around the back, he found the owner—a woman who was living in a guesthouse near the property line. They got to chatting and it turned out she was in the middle of a nasty divorce and hadn't made any payments on the house for six months. Here was a real motivated seller. Jim, like me, always believes in a win-win deal for both parties. He said, "Let me buy this from you, get you out from under the debt, and put some money in your pocket." She agreed. The property was worth (when fixed up) $1.7 million. Jim bought it for $1.3 million. He spent $50,000 making repairs and improvements. It took him forty-five days to renovate, another three weeks to sell, and fifteen days to close. Total cost: $1,350,000. Total time spent: eighty-one days. What did the property sell for? As I said, $1,700,000. How much did Jim make in eighty-one days? A tidy $350,000. Not bad for a few weeks of work.

Where do you find motivated sellers? First, look through your own local newspaper for ads that indicate the buyer is motivated to sell. Second, contact local real-estate agents to see if they have any clients likely to lower their asking price in exchange for a quick or even cash sale. Third, start attending meetings of your local real-estate investment club or association and talk to other investors. Often a property may not suit one investor because of timing, geography, or some other reason but would be perfect for you. Sharing and exchanging information is what Rich Idiots do to help one another become even richer.

Robert's Rule No. 3: Use as Little of Your Own Cash as Possible

Cash or Credit Partners

Use Other People's Money—as much of it as you can get.

This particular concept is very hard for RUBs to grasp and accept. Let me tell you a story that bears on that. I was in my early twenties. I'd been shadowing my first Rich Idiot mentor for over a year. Finally I plucked up the courage to purchase my very first property. I put on a pair of clean jeans, and off I went to the bank. Now remember, I came from the kind of home where if you didn't have the money for something, you simply didn't buy it. There were no credit cards. There were no loans. It was cash only. Maybe many of you also come from the same kind of background? Imagine me, this kid, sitting in a bank applying for my first loan. But I was confident, even though I didn't have any money. I figured I had really good credit. Guess what? Wrong. The loan officer typed in my Social Security number, looked at her computer screen, turned to me, and said, "Sorry, you don't qualify for a loan."

"Wait a minute," I protested. "I don't have any credit cards or loans or debt."

"That's the problem," she explained. "You have no credit history at all, so you don't get any credit."

Was that a wake-up call or what? How was I going to fund my first purchase? Well, I figured if banks weren't going to lend me any money, I'd have to find someone who would. And I did.

Now, here's the part that distinguishes Rich Idiots from RUBs. My new money partner said, "Looks like a good deal, Robert. I'll lend you the money you need, but when you sell the property I want half." It took me only a split second to figure out that half of an asset was better than no asset at all. I grabbed his terms and the property.

A few months later I sold it and split the cash with my partner, as agreed. My take? About $20,000. Not bad for a kid with no cash, no credit, and no experience.

A friend of mine tells a similar story. She was in her early twenties and had just graduated from college. But she knew she wasn't going to get rich working a job. So she spent two weeks looking for a house. This was several years ago, when the asking prices were much lower. She found a house she knew she could fix up and resell. The asking price was $62,500. The owner was willing to take a down payment of just under 5 percent, or $3,100. It might as well have been $3 million. All she could scrape together was $600.

But she got creative. She approached six of her sorority sisters and convinced them to each put up $500 for a 50 percent share in the profits. She put in $100 and kept her $500 for fixing it up. She didn't know it then, but she'd just formed a syndicate. Well, this story has a happy ending. She bought the property. Fixed it up. Sold it within sixty days for $84,500. She made $22,000. She paid back the initial investment and gave her partners $11,000 to split. She kept $11,000. Not bad for two months of work!

All too often I talk to people who, after finding a property and getting turned down by traditional lenders, are offered a second chance by a partner who wants half the pie. And what do these RUBs do? They walk away, usually muttering under their breath about the "greed of some people." They leave the money on the table. They leave an orphan asset. Who's hurt? The wannabe Rich Idiot. No money. No deal. No asset. No brains.

What's my advice? If you have a great deal, be grateful for a partner willing to let you ride his cash or credit. Do the Rich Idiot math. Half is better than zero. Got that?

Lease-Option and Lease-Purchase Strategies

The lease option and its kissin' cousin, the lease purchase, are two other successful strategies. The lease option is also called "lease with an option to buy." Here's how they work.

A lease option is partially a rental, partially a creative-financing strategy. You find a property, usually from a motivated seller, and sign a lease for a term of one to two years, or longer if possible. As part of the lease agreement there's an option clause allowing you to purchase the property during the term of the rental period for a previously agreed-upon price. But you don't have to buy it if you decide you don't want to.

Why is this a good deal for an up-and-coming Rich Idiot like you?

You don't need any up-front cash, and you can lock in a purchase price while riding the appreciation wave. So should you decide to exercise your option and purchase the property, it will probably have already gone up in price and you'll automatically have greater equity. There's another terrific advantage to you: Often you pay a little extra in rent, but that extra goes toward your down payment should you decide to buy, and it's locked in. So you've already got a kind of "forced asset-investment program" here.

Sellers also like this way of selling their property because they're getting rental income and a terrific tenant who's going to take very good care of the property, since they hope to purchase it.

A lease-purchase agreement is very similar except that you must purchase the property at the agreed-upon price at the end of your lease term.

Robert's Rule No. 4: Put Together a Real-Estate Dream Team

I can't emphasize this enough: You are *not* alone. Once again, in case you didn't hear me the first time: You are *not* alone. And if you *are* alone, you're not a Rich Idiot, you're a RUB.

Rich Idiots, as you already know, get successful through O.P. Power—the power, time, skills, information, and ideas of others. Acquiring your first real-estate assets is one of the best ways to begin building and refining your own dream team. "But, Robert, where am I going to find these people?" you ask. Simple. The same way you find anybody else: referrals. Ask people. You know that real-estate investors' meeting you're going to attend? That's a great place to find your Dream Team. You know that real-estate agent who keeps calling you? Another great resource to ask for Dream Team referrals. You get the idea, right?

Now, who's a dream team "must-have"?

1. One or two real-estate agents. But be careful. Not all real-estate agents understand or have experience in working with investors. Check prospective agents out. Make sure they have a positive track record, understand creative deals, and, best of all, own a couple of investment properties themselves.

2. A good title or escrow company. These are the people who'll do all your closings, and they're a huge resource. They can make things go smoothly, iron out any wrinkles, and protect you and your real-estate assets.

3. A real-estate attorney. No, your cousin isn't going to do it, unless his specialty is real estate. You need someone who understands investment real estate and isn't a deal breaker. Find the best one you can afford. You'll never regret it.

4. A mortgage banker can be a very valuable partner in your strategy for acquiring real-estate assets. This is the money person. Find a few good ones. Win their trust. Ask their advice. Keep them on your team.

5. A CPA who "gets it." Find one who works with real-estate investors and understands all the tax benefits due them.

This is your core Dream Team. As you acquire more properties and tenants, you may want to add a contractor, a handyman, and a property-management company.

Robert's Rule No. 5: Make Lots and Lots of Offers

Actually, now that I think of it, this should probably be Rule No. 1, because until you make an offer, you're a RUB. The minute you make that first offer, you've become (at least potentially) a Rich Idiot. The more offers you make, the bigger a Rich Idiot you'll become. After you've done your homework, of course. Set your goals. Assembled your Dream Team. And found your motivated buyers. Then there's only one thing left to do: Make an offer. Do a deal. Buy a property. What are you waiting for? Stop reading about becoming a Rich Idiot—go out, make that offer, and become a Rich Idiot!

Remember!
The more offers you make, the richer you'll get.

The Next Big Thing in Real Estate

One of the characteristics of Rich Idiots is their passion for discovering the "next big thing." Well, the next big thing in real estate isn't real at all—it's virtual. " Huh?" you say. "What do you mean, Robert?" Are you sitting down? This is going to astound you.

The Internet is rapidly becoming one of the fastest-growing real-estate markets, through special Web sites that allow users to buy and sell real estate. The real estate is virtual, but the money these Rich Idiots are making is real. Just a few clicks have brought real-estate wealth to thousands. One woman turned $10 into a million-dollar real-estate empire. Others are making impressive profits buying, selling, and developing real estate in virtual worlds like Second Life, Weblo, and Entropia.

Mortgage News Daily reports, "Second Life doesn't provide information on how many of its 6.5 million residents [now over 10 million] own real estate. . . . Residents may be motivated to acquire land to establish a business, and . . . residents are making real money every month providing goods and services from their virtual offices and stores."

I love this whole virtual concept and believe it's going to be the next huge wave for Internet entrepreneurs. In fact, come visit me on my very own Rich Idiot Island in Second Life. You'll have a chance to see firsthand how virtual real estate can work for you.

Here are some ways other Rich Idiots have already made real money in the new virtual real-estate land rush and how you can, too.

1. Become a virtual real-estate mogul.

Anshe Chung turned a modest investment of $10 into a million-dollar real-estate empire and became the virtual world's first real-estate millionaire in less than forty-eight months through Second Life, one of the fastest-growing virtual worlds, with over 7 million members and counting. Her remarkable story made the cover of *Business Week*.

2. Become a virtual real-estate agent—or buy from one.

Coldwell Banker is the first major real-estate company to open a virtual development, complete with virtual real-estate agents (called avatars), helicopter tours of available properties, and free furniture bonuses at closing. The brokerage firm has an inventory of five hundred homes in the Ranchero section of Second Life, one of the largest home developments in the virtual world.

3. Buy your own country, state, or city.

One of the newest and fastest-growing virtual real-estate sites is Weblo. TransWorldNews reports, "Weblo is the only parallel universe based on real properties, cities, and states. The site has sparked a virtual real-estate boom. California sold for $53,000 US. Florida sold for $18,047 . . . major cities and properties around the world have sold and resold for profit. The virtual mayor of Seattle sold his city for $2,000 after buying it for $40. Members flip virtual properties just like they do in the real world." A real-world real-estate agent owns more than seven hundred cities on Weblo, including Washington, D.C., and Lake Buena Vista in Florida (home of the Walt Disney World Resort). Courant.com reports, "He has earned hundreds of dollars off individual sites. . . . One user bought Las Vegas for $38, built up the page, and sold it for $430. The buyer then continued to work on the site and sold it for $2,300."

4. Buy and sell international real estate.

Harcourt, a New Zealand real-estate company, buys land and sells off parcels in the virtual world Second Life, with predicted returns running into five figures.

5. Virtual real-estate resales.

According to BBC News, the virtual property market is booming. "A gamer who spent £13,700 on an island that exists only in a computer game has recouped his investment, according to the game developers. The 23-year-old gamer known as Deathifier made the money back in under a year. The virtual Treasure Island he bought existed within the online role-playing game Project Entropia." CNET News.com reports on another Project Entropia real-estate investor who believes he can bring in more than $1.6 million a year in revenue—all on a onetime $100,000 investment.

6. Luxury apartment and condo rentals.

Virtual worlds have a thriving resale market in virtual condos and luxury apartments, many of which come completely furnished, feature amenities such as pools and ocean views, and sit on prime virtual real estate.

For more information on virtual real estate, go to The Next Big Thing at www.GetRichWithRobert.com.

Robert's Wrap-Up

Real or virtual, real estate is one of the three pillars of your Rich Idiot asset-acquisition strategy. So go out and buy something!

Your Rich Idiot Upside-Down Action Plan

1. Write down your real-estate goals.
2. Put together your Dream Team.
3. Make an offer today.

still secret no. 6

Invest in Stock Today

A dollar picked up in the road is more satisfaction to us than the
ninety-nine which we had to work for, and the money we won at faro
or in the stock market snuggles into our hearts the same way.
— MARK TWAIN

The Asset Known as Stock

We've talked a lot about assets and liabilities. Again, assets are things
you own or invest in that generally go up in value and bring you
wealth over time. Stocks and bonds are one of the four groups of assets
Rich Idiots accumulate, along with cash, real estate, and a business.
Here, then, is the upside-down Rich Idiot secret to investing in stocks
and bonds successfully.

Don't wait until you've paid off all your debts, put together a savings
account, set aside money for a college fund, and cleaned out the garage.

Take $100 and invest it in your first stock purchase—a $100 mutual fund. Do it today. With that first $100 purchase you've taken a gi-
ant step on the road to becoming a Rich Idiot.

What's your excuse for not becoming an investor right now? Are
you like those people who sit and wonder what stock to buy, or how to

begin? "I don't have any money to start," some of these people say. "How can I start investing in stocks when I don't have any savings or I can barely make ends meet?"

Or are you like a lot of other people, those who are overwhelmed by all the terms and financial words—loads, no-loads, IRAs, Roth IRAs, and so on—and afraid to act?

Of course, over time you'll begin to educate yourself and get comfortable with the terminology as well as the options available to you. But lack of education shouldn't stop you from making your very first stock investment. Systematic, regular, long-term stock investing will make you wealthy over time.

The Rich Idiot knows there's only one question worth asking, and that's "Will I start investing today?" If the answer is yes, congratulations! You're on your way!

Robert's Rules for Investing in Stocks

Over time I have developed a few surefire rules and have followed them myself with great success. I share them with you now. They are simple and easy to follow, and they work. Ready?

Rule No. 1: Losers Wait to Pick Winners

Don't for a moment think you can outsmart the market or the experts. Rich Idiots know there are people on Wall Street who have millions of dollars' worth of computer-analysis tools, reports, charts, graphs, and data. These are the experts. They track stocks day and night across global markets. And then there's you. You've maybe got the newspaper, a computer, and the hot tip the short-order cook at your local diner shared with you over breakfast this morning. Forget about it. Now, be aware, all of us want to pick the winner. We've all heard friends say, "Oh, I picked this stock and it went up 400 percent in a year. Isn't that fantastic?" But we need to remember that, just like in Vegas, people always tell you about the time they won, but they never tell you about the eight times they lost. If you're a hobbyist picking stocks part-time, you're not going to outsmart Wall Street. Period.

Rule No. 2: Start Your Stock-Investment Portfolio Today

It doesn't matter how much money you have to invest—$100 will get you into one of dozens of mutual funds. The secret is to do it. To pick up the phone, get online, set up an account, make the investment. Until you actually do it, you're not a Rich Idiot, you're a RUB.

Rule No. 3: Regular Investing Over Time Can Make You Wealthy

Regular stock investing over time can make you wealthy. Not investing over time will keep you where you are or worse. Get into the habit of logging on to your stock account and sending even the minimum deposit every month. You'll see how quickly your stock investment grows and multiplies. Over time, you'll probably do well, regardless of what class of investment you pick.

Rule No. 4: Use O.P. Power—Let the Pros Do It for You

What this means is, don't pick individual stocks. Find yourself a no-load mutual fund or money-management fund and let the pros make the stock picks for you. Remember, Rich Idiots use the power of other people. Nowhere is this more important than in your stock portfolio.

Rule No. 5: Use O.P. Power—Let the Pros Do It for You Again

The same holds true for deciding which mutual fund you're going to invest in. This is where you add a financial planner to your Dream Team and let him guide you. He'll do an analysis of your resources, but more important, he'll do a psychological analysis to determine your risk profile. He'll help you set an investment goal that fits your needs and the needs of your family. Then he'll guide you to the best investment vehicles that provide the best fit. I have just one word of warning here: Make sure you determine whether your investment adviser is an independent or whether he's associated with a financial organization that sells mutual funds and other financial products. I'm not saying that one is better than the other, but you need to be aware of any hidden agendas your adviser might have.

Rule No. 6: Never Invest Money You Can't Afford to Lose

Remember, the stock market can do only one of three things: go up, go down, or stay put. So if putting in that $100 means you're going to lose your home if you lose the money, don't invest it.

Rule No. 7: Invest for the Long Term, Not the Quick Buck

Your strategy, like the strategy for investing in real-estate assets, is to allow your stocks to mature so they can increase in value over time and bring in income. You need to be able to keep your money in your invested assets and allow time to do its work. Whenever a Rich Idiot invests in the stock market, he or she does it for the long term, to build wealth over time, not for the next ninety days, six months, or even year. For a Rich Idiot, the long term means five years or more. As Warren Buffett, the ultimate investor, says, "Only buy something that you'd be perfectly happy to hold if the market shut down for ten years."

Rule No. 8: Be a Conservative Investor

I have a great story to illustrate this point. I was in training at Goldman Sachs on Wall Street when one day a gentleman came to speak to our class. I was about twenty-five years old and thought, "Gee, I'm smart. I'm going to pick stocks and beat everybody and beat the market." I was confident and ready to take some big risks to prove just how smart I was. But this man said something that made a lasting impression on me and dramatically changed my own investment strategy on the spot—a change I never regretted. He was about sixty-five years old and a billionaire investor. (This was a few years ago, when billionaires were few and far between and a billion dollars really meant something.) This is what he said to all of us young hotshots: "Look, a lot of you are young right now. You think you're smart and you think you know a lot of stuff, but you don't. When you get older and wiser with years of experience and see all the stocks that go down and all the risks and all the gambling that people do, you'll at some point in your investment career become very conservative. So you might as well get conservative now and save yourselves thirty, forty, fifty years of investment aggravation and stress. Invest in good stocks and good companies. Do it for the long term, because no other investment strategy works as well."

And you know what? That guy had a billion dollars and I didn't. So as a wannabe Rich Idiot back then, I decided to take his advice. I got rid of my little penny stocks and funky tip-of-the-week stocks, which had mostly all gone down anyway. I changed my strategy from "get rich quick and risky" to "get rich slow and safe." I was in for the long run. I wanted to build assets like this billionaire. And the strategy has worked for me all these years.

Rule No. 9: Avoid Hot Tips—They Cool Off Really, Really Fast

Let me tell you what happened when my good friend Rich called with a hot tip. Rich worked on Wall Street and was one of the young Turks on the move. I never listened to his tips, and I must admit I did feel a twinge of "what if" every time I declined. Except this one time. That morning Rich called and said, "Robert, you've got to invest in this one. It's a real winner. It's seven cents a share; you could buy fifty thousand shares and make a fortune." I wasn't completely convinced. "What kind of stock is it? What's the company? What's the stock doing?" I asked. "It doesn't matter," Rich replied. "Just buy it." There was something very insistent in Rich's voice, so this time I took the plunge. I bought 50,000 shares at 7 cents a share and wrote a check for $3,500.

Within days it went to 12 cents; then it climbed to 15 cents and then 30 cents, and suddenly it was at 90 cents.

I started flipping out. I had just made a lot of money in only a couple of days, and that made me nervous. I called Rich and asked, "What should I do, hold or sell?" Without hesitation he said, "Hold on. It's going to go to $1.20 a share. I'm sure it is."

This time I didn't take Rich's advice. I got scared, and at 90 cents a share I sold. I made some good money. It was fantastic. My $3,500 investment had turned into $45,000 in just a matter of days.

So what happened to the stock after I bailed? Sure enough, the next day it rose to $1.20, just like Rich had said it would. And then it crashed. When it landed it was selling for 8 cents a share. As Ralph Seger, founder of one of the most successful trading companies of all time, has said, "You can never predict when that unknown torpedo will come out of the dark and smash the price of a stock."

I got lucky. And I learned my lesson. No more roller-coaster rides. I was going to take the billionaire route to riches. Slow and steady wins the wealth.

Rule No. 10: Avoid Investing in Start-up Stocks

Here's why: 70 to 80 percent of start-up companies go out of business. Start-up stocks are not for Rich Idiot investors. Generally, the risk outweighs the rewards, and most Rich Idiots prefer to invest, not gamble.

Warning!
Never invest in anything you don't understand completely.
This includes all aspects of the investment
you are contemplating.

Rule No. 11: Use the Asset-Allocation
Strategy for Your Stock Portfolio

In this context, asset allocation means not putting all your stocks in one basket. You shouldn't invest all your stock-investment dollars in a single industry or company; you should spread the risk around. If one of your stocks fails to perform or, worse, plummets, you can offset the negative result with positive performances from the others you've purchased.

Let me tell you a story about a friend in Nashville who started an Internet company and rode the dot-com boom all the way to the top and then all the way back down to the bottom. He started with a $30,000 investment budget and three employees. Within one year the firm had grown to two hundred employees. A few months later he'd raised $80 million. "Robert," he told me one day, "I'm worth over $200 million." He was on the front page of the local paper. He was a huge success. I was really proud of him.

I saw him about six months later, and guess what his net worth was? Zero.

"At least I got to ride the ride," he told me. "I went from zero to a couple of hundred million dollars to zero in two years," he said. "It was amazing. I learned a lot." But he had nothing to show for it other than the ability to give a great seminar on asset allocation.

What should he have done? Obviously, he should have taken some of that wealth and put it off to the side.

So what do Rich Idiots know? As soon as they start collecting assets, they take some of those assets and diversify into other assets. There is no such thing as zero risk. Remember, even in the United States, banks were closed and many stocks became worthless. Broad allocation of assets among categories is critical.

Rule No. 12: Invest in Tax-Free Vehicles

When you make money in stocks and bonds, you'll eventually have to pay taxes on your gains, so you want to hold your stocks in tax-free vehicles as much as possible. One of the best ways to do that is to boost your 401(k) contributions. The same thing goes for self-directed IRAs and pension plans. A good investment adviser can help you figure out which mix of these will work best and assist you in setting them up correctly.

Rule No. 13: Monitor Your Stock Portfolio

I recommend taking a look at the performance of your stock portfolio every month or once a quarter—certainly every year. Stock-portfolio goals are important and need to be monitored. I'm not saying you should make rapid changes, but I am saying you need to be aware of what's going on so you can react accordingly—get advice or move your investment dollars around. I look at my assets every week. Every business I'm involved in, every asset, I look at it weekly. Every Friday I take fifteen or thirty minutes and look at all my inflows and outflows and make sure they're meeting my goals.

Rule No. 14: Consolidate Your Accounts

I like to place all my accounts with one brokerage or one bank. You might say, "But, Robert, that's not diversification." You'd be wrong, though, because my accounts are diversified and my investments are diversified. Sure, a lot of people get reports from, say, eight different stock companies and three brokerage accounts. I like to keep things very simple. One organization. One report.

Rule No. 15: Remember O.P. Power—Use a Professional Financial Planner

I think everybody should sit down with a professional financial planner, even if they're making only $20,000 or $30,000 a year. There are companies that will determine what kind of assets you need to acquire and help you get started. Get an expert to help you determine how to best use tax savings and tax-deferral vehicles such as IRAs, self-directed IRAs, pension plans, insurance, and annuities—also which asset allocation is best for you and your family to meet your goals.

Your Rich Idiot Upside-Down Action Plan

1. Make an appointment with a financial planner—and keep it.
2. Pick up the phone right now and make your first mutual-fund stock investment.

chapter **10**

still secret no. 6

Start Your Own Business

My son is now an "entrepreneur." That's what
you're called when you don't have a job.
— TED TURNER

Become a Rich Idiot: Start Your Very Own Business

Here's the third asset pillar to support your new Rich Idiot life. You'll
need all three to go from RUB to Rich Idiot and stay there. Let's take
a quick look at the three legs to this Rich Idiot stool:

- Real estate
- Stocks and bonds
- Business

Remember assets? Assets are those things you own or invest in
that generally go up in value and bring you wealth over time. Your
own business, not somebody else's business, is one of those assets Rich
Idiots accumulate, along with real estate and stock.

The reality is, most Rich Idiots who are truly, truly wealthy got
that way by starting their own business. If you want to become a Rich

Idiot, guess what? You're going to have to start your own business someday, so you might as well start it right now.

I'm hearing that RUB "but, Robert" whine again. Forget about it. I've heard all the reasons why starting a business is not a good idea. I've read all the stats about the start-up failure rate. I know all the excuses: "I don't have the time, the skills, the money, the support . . . " and on and on and on. I've listened to all the naysayers, the economists, the pollsters. For every business start-up horror story you've heard, I've heard ten. And you know what? I'm sticking to my Rich Idiot guns. If you want to be a Rich Idiot, start your own business part-time or full-time. Period. End of story.

Remember!
You're always building someone's
business—build your own.

Employees Don't Get to Become Billionaires— Bosses Do

I just spent a really fun hour going over *Forbes*'s "Special Report: The 400 Richest Americans," all of whom are worth over a billion dollars. You know what I noticed? Not one works for somebody else. There's not a single employee in the bunch. Pretty compelling validation for my "own your own business" thesis.

But I wasn't satisfied just looking at billionaires. I wanted to throw even more proof at you that owning your own business is the way to get rich. Ready? According to U.S. Census data, there are over 4 million households in America with a net worth above $1 million (excluding equity in their own home). The data goes on to show that of these 4 million millionaire households, 30 percent achieved this success by owning a small business. If 1.2 million American households can become

Rich Idiots by owning a business and over 400 Americans can become billionaires by working for themselves, don't you think you can, too?

There's more proof. Wealth statistics show that it's the self-employed who are America's wealthy. According to information from the latest Survey of Consumer Finances, the average net worth of a family in which the head of the household works for someone else is $65,000. Compare this to $352,300 for the average net worth of a family in which the head of the household is self-employed. What this means is that on average people who are self-employed—have their own businesses—boast a net worth that's nearly five and a half times greater than people who are employees. Put another way: RUBs have less, Rich Idiots have more. Which would you rather be?

Fail First

One of the most common reasons people cite for not starting their own business is fear—fear of failure. That's crazy, because failure is something to embrace and celebrate. It's one of the most significant upside-down components of starting your own business and striking it rich: Fail first.

There's plenty of validation for this surprising point of view. Jude Wanniski, a political economist, wrote, "All success is the result of failure. It takes repeated attempts to succeed before success is achieved. Just think how many times you tried to eat with a spoon before you got the hang of it, let alone a knife and fork. Success, of course, is 'better' than failure, but success is not possible without failure."

BusinessWeek took up this theme in a recent article, "How Failure Breeds Success." "Everyone fears failure," says the magazine. "But breakthroughs depend on it. The best companies embrace their mistakes and learn from them." Practically every major corporation has failed at one time or another, but one of the best examples of celebrating failure is the failure party thrown by Intuit, Inc. "Intuit recently celebrated an adventurous marketing campaign that failed," reports

BusinessWeek. "The company had never targeted young tax filers before, and in early 2005 it tried to reach them through an ill-fated attempt to combine tax-filing drudgery with hip-hop style. Through a Web site called RockYourRefund.com Intuit offered young people discounts to travel site Expedia Inc. and retailer Best Buy and the ability to deposit tax refunds directly into prepaid Visa cards issued by hip-hop mogul Russell Simmons." The whole project was a flop. What did the chairman of Intuit do to the team that failed? According to the article, "In front of some 200 Intuit marketers, the team received an award from Intuit Chairman Scott Cook." The chairman realized that to be successful, you will fail sometimes, and the question to ask is, what can I do next time to do it better?

Remember!
Only failures become successes.
Failure isn't an option—it's part of your success process.

Having the courage to fail isn't just something spouted by the big boys of corporate America. Failure is an integral part of entrepreneurial success as well. Debbi Fields, the founder of Mrs. Fields Cookies, said, "The important thing is not being afraid to take a chance. Remember, the greatest failure is not to try."

But there's an even more important part of failure than having one. It's shutting down and never trying again. So you failed at your last attempt to pass a test, lose a size, get a date, start a business—so what? It's only fatal if you never try again. "Failure doesn't count," says motivator Frank Burford. "If you accept this, you'll be successful. What causes most people to fail is that after one failure, they'll stop trying." So if you've tried to start your own business and failed, terrific! You've gained valuable experience and are now a member of a very elite club, along with every single Rich Idiot out there. We've all failed. But we all tried again.

You're Sweating the Workout but Your
Boss Is Getting Your Six-Pack Abs

Think of it this way: As long as you're working for someone else, it's like you're at the gym every day doing a major workout. You're sweating. You're doing all the heavy lifting. But all that effort is going to build a great set of pecs or abs for your employer. If you're going to do all that work and put in all those hours, you should be the one getting all the benefits. That's Rich Idiot thinking.

Here's All You Need to Know About
Starting Your Own Business

I know there are hundreds of books out there filled with thousands of pages regarding how to pick your business, start your business, capitalize your business, manage your business, expand your business—the list goes on. In fact, there are so many books that you could spend the next twenty years learning all about business without ever starting one. And until you do, you'll never become a Rich Idiot. It's like riding a bike. You can read about it. You can look at pictures of other people riding bikes. You can go to school and study the physics of motion, the geometry of wheels, and the properties of rubber. But until you climb up on that shiny new bike, you're not riding. You may be a little wobbly; you may need training wheels; you may want someone to run alongside the first few times you get on. But in the end, to be able to ride a bike, you've got to be the one pumping those pedals. There's no other way to learn how. The same holds true for having your own business.

There are, however, a few simple things that can get you started right away.

Robert's Rule No. 1: Don't Do a Big, Complicated Business Plan

I have a friend who spent $50,000 on a professionally prepared business plan. It was over a hundred pages long and came in a very pretty folder. But what did she really have? She had a $50,000 hole in her checkbook and a bunch of paper. Did she have a business? No. Another sad business-plan story involves an acquaintance who spent $20,000 in business-plan consulting fees over a three-year period for a business that has yet to get off the ground. In both of these examples the budding entrepreneurs developed a business plan that was so enormous and complex that they got frustrated even before they began.

Me, I follow the KISS approach—Keep It Simple, Stupid.

I've launched several successful businesses. I've partnered in many successful businesses. And I have one simple rule about business plans: Keep it simple and brief. In fact, the specific business plan I used to launch my first real-estate empire is shown on page 221. It's the model I've used for every business I've launched since then. It has only five parts. It's all you'll need. Go ahead—feel free to use it yourself. Oh, and one more thing. If this format takes you longer than an hour to flesh out, you're still in RUB mode.

Let's walk through each one of these five elements so you can see how simple but powerful they are. Also, you should know that when I started out I had a full-time job. I was working for somebody else—just like you. If I could find the time to start a business, so can you.

Mission Statement

The first thing to write down is your mission statement. This is where you really get to think about your values. About what's important to you. What you stand for. This is where you get to write down your dream, your vision. Your mission statement should always be about more than just the money. As Henry Ford, one of the greatest entrepreneurs, said, "If money is your hope for independence you will never have it. The only real security that a man will have in this world

Robert's One-Page Rich Idiot Business Plan

My Mission Statement: I want to provide quality low-income housing, treat my tenants like valued customers, and make an ethical profit.

My Time Commitment: I'm going to stick with my plan to do real estate for five years, no matter what happens.

My Goal: I want to become financially independent by obtaining ten properties within three years.

My Activities: I'm going to call ten to twenty investors a week. I'm going to take one investor to lunch every week. I'm going to meet two new investors every other week. I'm going to call five to fifteen deal makers and make two offers a week.

My Schedule: Wednesdays 4:00 P.M. to 7:00 P.M., Saturdays 10:00 A.M. to 3:00 P.M., and Monday, Tuesday, and Thursday evenings for forty-five minutes.

is a reserve of knowledge, experience, and ability." Like Henry says, don't make it *just* about the money.

Time Commitment

Next, write down your time commitment. You have to set a time limit on your efforts. You've all heard the saying that an overnight success takes twenty years. Well, the good news is that it doesn't take twenty years—but it does take more than ten minutes.

When I declared, "I'm in this for five years," that was one of the smartest things I ever did. Here's why: For the first month nothing much happened. I kept at it. Nothing much happened for the first year. I still kept at it. Nothing much happened for the second year. Like the Energizer Bunny I just kept on going, following my one-page plan. By year three, people started calling *me*. Opportunities started landing in *my* lap. My business took off. I was on my way.

It takes time to build up momentum and get things going. That's why specifying a time horizon is so critical. It forced me to give my fledgling business the necessary time to grow and flourish.

Remember!
Money is time.

Most people set unrealistic time goals for themselves and their business. Then when they can't achieve them, they quit. But, often, after you've been doing something for one, two, or three years, there's liftoff. That's when people start noticing and saying, "You're so lucky, that deal just fell into your lap." Well, it's not luck. It's harvesttime for all the seeds you've planted over a long growing season. During a start-up's beginning weeks, months, and years Rich Idiots are getting smarter, stronger, better. When riches come, they're ready for them.

Financial Goal

Next is your financial goal. Make it as specific as possible, and always add what you're going to do to achieve it. It's pointless to write, "I'm going to make a million dollars," unless you also spell out how you're going to do it. Are you going to buy real estate or stocks, bake a zillion pies, buy a commercial airline . . . what exactly are you going to do?

Activities

You can't skip the fourth step, planning purposeful activities. This is important. One of those *Forbes* billionaires, forty-eight-year-old Mark

Cuban, was asked, "What's more important, the idea or the execution?" He didn't hesitate: "Execution. Everyone has ideas." You must do something every day to bring you closer to your business goal. For business, this is where the rubber meets the road. Without a plan of action, all you'll ever have is great ideas—you and the other millions of RUBs out there. With a plan of action, you're in Rich Idiot territory.

Remember!
Idea = RUB

Idea + Action = Rich Idiot

Schedule

The final element of the business plan I'm advocating is discipline. You have no boss. There's no time clock to punch. It's up to you. You must set hours and stick to them. When you add up the number of hours you typically have to spare every week for building a business, you'll be surprised to see that it's about seven or eight. Most people think you need hundreds of hours to launch a business. Not true. You can launch a successful business in just an hour a day—but it's got to be every day and a full hour.

You know, there were many, many times during those first critical years of my business that I felt like quitting. I endured a lot of bad days. But I regularly pulled out my plan and reread it, reaffirming my five-year commitment. I can't tell you how glad I am that I stuck with it, that I did it every day, and that I stayed true to my mission statement and my goal.

Here's the scheduling form I developed to track my own time. The only true asset you have in life is your time. How are you spending it? I like to track my time for business in fifteen-minute increments.

Robert's Time-Tracking Form

Activity	Time spent	Has it or will it make money? How much?	Do I enjoy doing it? Can I get someone else to do it?
_____	_____	_____	_____
_____	_____	_____	_____
_____	_____	_____	_____

And so on . . .

Robert's Rule No. 2: Focus

I get calls every day from the students I coach, and here's what a few of them might say: "Robert, this stuff doesn't work. I'm not making any money. I'm frustrated. I'm upset."

"What *activities* are you doing?" I ask, with heavy emphasis on the word *activities*. But I know the answer even before I hear their list—a list that could choke a horse.

"I've been really busy. I'm working all the time."

"I've been reading your book. I read it three times, Robert."

"I met with twelve people, like you said."

"I went to a bunch of meetings."

"I went to a training session."

"I set up my office."

"I read the paper and circled ten ads."

"I made my five phone calls. But I'm telling you, nothing's working."

"Have you bought anything? Have you sold anything?" I ask. Until you actually make that offer, sign that client, sell your product, or buy that piece of real estate or stock, nothing *is* going to happen for you. At the end of the day, you have to ask yourself, "Is what I'm doing purposeful activity, something that's making me money, or is it busy-work?"

One of the businesses I entered into was a network marketing company. I got the idea of focusing on activities that were quickly profitable. If I signed people up and sent in the paperwork, I got a great big fat check. If I didn't sign people up and send in the applications, no money arrived. What was my focus? I didn't spend hours studying compensation plans, making endless to-do lists, going to meetings, or organizing and reorganizing my paper clips. Rather, I focused on signing people up.

What are you spending most of *your* time doing? Make yourself a time log and write down everything you do, hour by hour, for a week. I guarantee that you'll be shocked at how much time you're wasting on activities that aren't bringing you any closer to your Rich Idiot goal.

That's what Rich Idiots do. They focus. What's your focus? If you don't have one you'll be stuck spinning your wheels, doing "stuff," and never making Rich Idiot–sized money.

Robert's Rule No. 3: What *It* Is Doesn't Matter— What Matters Is That You Love It

Bob Dylan got it right when he said, "A man is a success if he gets up in the morning and gets to bed at night, and in between he does what he wants to do."

I'm asked all the time, "Robert, what's the best business for me to start?" And my answer's always the same:

"The best business for you to start is the one you love."

Think about what you love to do, then do it. It doesn't matter if your specialty is coffee like Starbucks, burgers like McDonald's, jewelry like Cartier, watches like Rolex, or flowers like 1-800-Flowers. As Anita Roddick, founder of the Body Shop, says, "Success to me is not about money or status or fame, it's about finding a livelihood that brings me joy and self-sufficiency and a sense of contributing to the world." Right on, Anita. For those of you reading this, the lesson is as follows: Find yourself something to love . . . success and money will follow.

It surely came to my friend and old neighbor Garth Brooks, the famous country singer. Now he's sold more records than almost anyone but the Beatles and is one of the most successful artists of all time, yet he started out working in a boot store in Nashville. Back then he told everyone that his passion was music. He measured feet and stacked boxes, and all the time he kept saying how his one big love was songs. He went to over twenty record companies with his own compositions and was thrown out of each, not once but three and four times. Didn't matter. Garth knew what he was going to do and stuck with his passion until he became a success.

What's your passion? What's that one thing you'd love to do—even if nobody paid you to do it? That's your answer. That's the business you should start.

Let's Take a Break and Look at Your Job vs. Your Own Business Scenario

I can hear all of you right about now. You want your own business so badly, but you've still got that employee mentality. "Robert, I'd love to start my own business, but I need my job. I've got tenure. I've got fifteen years invested in the company. I'm up for a promotion. I've got my pension. I've got job security."

And you know what I say? There's no such thing as job security. It doesn't matter how many years you've got invested, what kind of a promotion you've been promised, or how much your boss respects you. The reality is, you could lose your job tomorrow. It happens all the time. Your company goes under or gets sold. Your boss gets fired and office politics dictate that you follow him right out that door. The pension fund goes bankrupt. Call it what you want: Downsizing. Asset redistribution. Reengineering. The result is the same. One day you have a job; the next day you don't. That's not what Rich Idiots call security. Job security—Rich Idiot-style—is you at the wheel, in control of your income, your life, and your future. That's real security.

Remember!
YOU are the only job security you've got.

Robert's Rule No. 4: Revenues Lead Expenses

What does this mean? In Rich Idiot-speak, it means don't spend what you don't have. You don't need that fancy desk, huge office, or ten employees, at least not until your business is making a ton of money. What *do* you need? Let me tell you what I've got—and I'm making millions. I've got a cell phone, a laptop, a home office, and an assistant. That's it. I subcontract and joint venture almost everything. I can run my business from South Beach, New York City, South America, a cruise—and so can you.

Robert's Rule No. 5: Don't Work Hard

I'll go even further than that and say, "If you work too hard, you're a RUB and will stay a RUB." Rich Idiots regularly take time off from their business. They schedule a day or a week where they can go off by themselves and think about where they are and where they're going. When was the last time you took a day just to think about yourself, your needs, your plans? If you haven't taken a mental retreat in the past thirty days you've got my permission to go do it. That day or week off will do more to help you become a Rich Idiot than all the sixty- or eighty-hour weeks combined. You'll come back refreshed, restored, and invigorated—and so will your business.

The other part of the "Don't work hard" Rich Idiot business

formula is this: If you can't leave your business for an extended period of time, you're not yet a Rich Idiot. If you leave for three months, will your business crash and burn? Will it be there when you get back? Can your business run without you?

Remember!
It's not how hard you work.
It's how smart you work.

I learned this lesson in a very unusual way. I was busy building up my business, working hard and giving it my all. One day my wife, who was from Europe, where everyone takes four- to six-week vacations, told me she'd booked us on a flight to visit her family for a whole month. Nothing I said would get her to change her mind. We were going, and that was it. So I found someone to answer my phone, someone else to pick up my mail, someone to pay my bills, and someone to take the deposits to the bank. Now, here's the weird part: I was worried sick that I'd come back and find I had no business left, that I'd have to start all over again. But guess what? I made more money that month than I'd ever made, and things were running more smoothly. Now I regularly take off three or more months, and my business is flourishing. If I can do it, so can you.

Remember!
Reward yourself for every success, no matter
how small, along the way.

Out of This World

You don't have to limit your business to this world—you can make money in the virtual world, too. Remember how we talked about virtual worlds such as Second Life in Chapter 8?

A virtual world is an online world in which you can buy and sell stuff, start any kind of business, make money, and never leave home.

Virtual worlds are springing up all over the Internet, so they're simply a click away on your own computer. And the best part of these virtual worlds is that you can make real money. Take a look. According to *The Next Big Thing*, by E. M. Kaye, people spend over $1.5 billion on virtual items every year, buying and selling virtual goods such as furniture for virtual houses and clothing and jewelry for their digital alter egos (also known as avatars). They party at virtual clubs, gamble in virtual casinos, travel in virtual cars, and buy and sell virtual real estate. And all this virtual "stuff" is paid for with real-world money.

- As previously mentioned, Second Life is one of the fastest-growing virtual worlds, with almost 10 million residents and a growth rate in the double digits. Millions of dollars change hands on this economic platform every month.
- Tencent, one of the largest Internet portals in China, with over 250 million active user accounts, generated over $100 million in the first quarter of 2007. Incredibly, over 65 percent of this revenue came from virtual goods.
- Gaia Online conducts over 50,000 person-to-person auctions and organizes a million message board posts a day—making it the third-largest auction site and the second-largest message board on the Internet. In addition to garnering massive credit card sales, it has a staff of people whose only job is to open envelopes filled with cash payments for virtual products.

It's estimated that the number of virtual worlds doubles every two years, so there are literally millions of new opportunities for building businesses. And you don't have to be a geek or even computer savvy.

Just Do It!

I could finish with long checklists of things to do before starting your own business, including rules to follow, forms to fill out, consultants to consult, and so on—but I'm not going to. You've already got everything you need. You've got the passion, the drive, the desire, and the information. You've also got me, Robert, your Rich Idiot friend, mentor, and ally. You've got my entire team to help you. You've got my Web site, www.GetRichWithRobert.com, to supply you with huge daily doses of information and inspiration. You've got it all.

The only thing left for me to do is tell you to start. Right now. Just do it!

Rich Idiot Upside-Down Action Plan

1. Write your simple business plan.
2. Decide what business feeds your passion. That's the business you're going to start.

chapter 11

secret no. 7

Act

The best way to predict the future is to create it.
— PETER DRUCKER

Remember These Rich Idiots?

Back at this book's beginning there was the guy who whizzed past in a brand-new Cadillac or Porsche, flashing his Rolex. You recognized him as the idiot who'd flunked out of your school, while you'd studied hard and earned straight A's. Remember asking, as you sat in your eight-year-old car, checking the time on your knockoff watch, "If I'm so smart, how come that idiot's rich and I'm not?"

Want to know the answer? Because that guy wasn't really worried about straight A's. After he flunked out he got a job waiting tables. He smiled a lot. He got great tips. The day you graduated high school he bought his first duplex. The day you received your ten-year corporate pen he was already retired. What made him a Rich Idiot? Action.

Remember picking up your local newspaper and recognizing the guy in the photo as that kid who couldn't make change? Now he's all grown up, shaking hands with the governor and running a billion-dollar company. You, on the other hand, always got your sums right. But the only person who ever shakes your hand is the greeter at Wal-Mart.

Remember asking, "If I'm so dependable, how come that idiot's rich and I'm not?"

Want to know? While you were busy with your math homework, this kid got a bunch of his loser friends together, set up shop in his old man's garage, and started churning out computer programs, talking to venture capitalists, and making sales. What made him a Rich Idiot? Action, again.

Remember the moment when you realized that the guy giving that seminar and tossing hundred-dollar bills into the crowd was the son of your mom's neighbor in Queens? He was that lanky kid with the baggy pants who was always borrowing money off everyone because he never had a dime. Remember wondering how he ended up with all the money and you ended up trying to make ends meet every month?

Want to know how that happened? He got really good at borrowing. He borrowed himself into his first piece of real estate, then into his first business. He became skilled at using O.P. Power. He asked for money. He asked for better deals. He asked for help. He took action. What did you do?

How about this one: Remember reading that story in *People* magazine about the kid you used to babysit? The one whose clothes always clashed who now owns an online fashion empire.

Remember wondering, "How come that idiot's got this terrific creative full life, and I'm standing at the checkout counter worrying about the price of a couple of magazines?"

Let me tell you why. She spent her nights creating her designs and her days stitching them into something tangible on her mother's old sewing machine. She took her creations around to every design studio and store in Manhattan. When they slammed the door in her face, she learned how to set up a Web site and started selling on the Internet. What was her secret? She took action. She did whatever was necessary to make her dream come true.

Remember how thrilled you were to be promoted to vice president of something or other until you recognized the keynote speaker and his family at your company's annual meeting? He never made it through school, and she got pregnant and dropped out, too. Now they've got this great family and an international philanthropic organization. They give away more in an hour than you earn in a year. Remember asking, "If I work so hard and I'm so smart, why is the universe doling out these lavish gifts to people who broke all the rules?"

I'm guessing that by now you know the answer. These people got an idea and then they acted on it.

That moxie is what all Rich Idiots have. That's their biggest secret. It's not that they had the best idea. It's not that they got all the breaks. It's not that they could call on support, or possessed a great education or a trust fund. No. What they all had was a conviction that they needed to take action.

Nobody Really Knows What's Going On

I know that a lot of you never take action because you're afraid you don't know enough—you're not ready. So what happens? You spend months, even years preparing yourself, learning, researching, and trying to anticipate every single thing that could happen. Why? Because you don't want to admit how much you don't know. You don't want to look like an idiot. But guess what? That's exactly what you look like when you don't act.

I want to reassure you about something and erase your fears: Rich Idiots don't know everything. In fact, most of the time they don't know what to do at all. But they take their best shot anyway.

I'm going to tell you a story, and I hope I don't get into trouble for it. It was told to me by the chairman of one of the most powerful financial organizations on Wall Street. The incident happened in the late 1980s behind closed doors, and it involved a dozen of America's most prestigious banks and financial institutions and the powerful men who ran them. My friend was one of those men that day.

The stock market was crashing. The American economy was in

trouble. So the Federal Reserve chairman arranged for the heads of the ten most important banks and investment houses to be on a conference call with him early the next morning, to decide what to do. Think about this: an all-star gathering of experts from California to New York in their offices at the crack of dawn to save the country.

All except my friend. He left home in plenty of time to get in on the call, but when he arrived at his office he found he'd forgotten the security garage remote control and couldn't get into the building. You'd think this guy would be organized enough to remember a little thing like a clicker. But no. So now he's sitting in his car waiting for someone to come along and open the underground garage.

He finally entered the building and got on the call. Here's how it went.

"Hi, Harry, what do you think we should do?" asked the chairman of the Federal Reserve.

"Don't have a clue, Mr. Chairman," replied Harry.

"How about you, Chuck, got any ideas?"

"Wouldn't want to say," replied Chuck, the head of one of the biggest banks in the country.

"Edward, let me hear what you think."

"Well, if the truth be told, I'm not thinking much."

And that's how it went, around and around the conference call, with not one Rich Idiot having a clue about what to do.

Until finally somebody said, "Hey, let's just, you know, put some more money into the system and hope it works." Thank God somebody made a decision and took some action, because it did work and stability returned to the financial markets.

My purpose in telling this story is to show that even Rich Idiots don't know what they're doing sometimes. They're making it up as they go along. Just like everybody. Just like you.

But there's one striking difference: You think the heads of corporations, the best, the brightest, the smartest who are in control, know exactly what they are doing. Sometimes they don't, but at least they make a decision and take some action. Rich Idiots do *something*. They take action. These experts were faced with something they'd never encountered before, and they had to take action. At first, just like everybody typically does, they said, "We don't know what to do." But even not knowing, they did something. They acted.

Are you frozen? Worried that you don't know what to do? It doesn't matter. Just *act* as if you do.

Even Rich Idiots Were Scared the First Day of Kindergarten

I want to tell you how I conquered my own fear and finally summoned up the courage to take some action. It's a story about kids and kindergarten and law school.

I'll never forget my first day of law school. (Yes, I finally got in—don't ask me how I made it.)

Anyway, it was the first day and there were about four hundred of us—the best and the brightest—all scared to death. Then Dean Epstein, a world-renowned lawyer and teacher, rose to address the class.

"Hey, everybody! I want you all to relax," he said in his Texas drawl.

We sat there all thinking, "Yeah, right—we're not going to relax again until the day we graduate, three years from now." The fact was, every one of us was terrified. We were afraid the workload would be too heavy, afraid we wouldn't be at the top of the class, afraid we'd be ridiculed by our fellow students, afraid we'd flunk out. This was one quivering mass of frightened law students.

"Do you remember your first day of kindergarten?" asked Epstein. "Remember how you clung to your mother's hand because you were scared to death? You were terrified you wouldn't make it through kindergarten. But you know what, you made it through. You went on to elementary school—same terror that first day. Then there was the first day in the big leagues—junior high—and more fear. Then you went on to high school. Remember how scared you were that first day, looking at all those huge seniors? Then suddenly you were a senior yourself. Then you were back to being a frightened freshman in college . . . and now here you are, experiencing another first day, and you're scared all over again. But I can get you over your fear. Just think of it as the first day of kindergarten, only seventeen years later. You made it through then, and you'll make it through now."

You could hear a collective sigh of relief from four hundred first-day law students.

So if you're scared to act because it's all new and unknown, ask yourself this: "Am I better at my job today than I was the first day I was hired?" Trust that you'll get better at investing, better at real estate, better at starting and running a business, better at becoming a Rich Idiot the more you do it. John Lennon may have said it best: "The unknown is what it is. . . . Accept that it's unknown, and it's plain-sailing."

Take Care of Yourself First

Here's an important and very upside-down principle: When you act, act to take care of yourself first. Pay yourself first. Rest yourself first. Reward yourself first. If you don't take good care of your primary asset—you—you won't be able to take care of all the other people who will come to depend on you as you become more and more wealthy.

I learned this "self-love" lesson the hard way. I'm your typical Rich Idiot. I love what I do so much that I was working nonstop, helping people, managing my charities, traveling all over the world speaking, running my businesses, and buying and selling properties, until one day my good friend and doctor, Richard Hirsch, asked, "Robert, do you like to help people?"

"You know I do," I answered.

"How would you like to help people for another twenty, thirty, forty, or sixty years?"

"That would be terrific," I replied. "How do I do that?"

"By taking better care of yourself right now," he shot back. "By not taking care of yourself, by not putting your own health and rest first, you're shaving valuable years off your life. If you're dead from stress and overwork, you're no use to anyone. Think how many more people you could help if you lived a longer life."

I finally got it. By taking care of myself I was going to be able to take better care of others for a lot longer. I had never looked at it that way. Like most of you, I was raised to believe that putting yourself first is somehow selfish. But Rich Idiots know that putting yourself first is a purely unselfish act.

So do it. Start taking care of you, right now. Act on it.

Start at the End

Here's another piece of Rich Idiot upside-down wisdom: Start at the end. Rich Idiots always begin every project, every investment, and every action with the desired result in mind. It's clear outcomes you want. You must make sure that your destination is reachable. Ask yourself these three critical questions:

1. What result do I want?
2. Is the result possible?
3. How badly do I want it?

Here's what I do. I decide on the result I want from every single activity. If I'm going to make a phone call, I decide what I want to have happen by the time I hang up. If I'm going to a meeting, I decide what I want to have accomplished when the meeting is over.

I also determine whether what I want is possible or just pie in the blue sky. Am I in the ballpark or way out past left field? Can I accomplish my goal in a reasonable amount of time? What other re-sources besides myself will I need to bring in? Sometimes the answers aren't what I'm looking for, so I adjust and begin the process again.

Finally, I ask myself how badly I want the result. Do I really want to close on that deal? Is that property the right one? Have I asked my

Dream Team for advice on a particular investment? Do I like the person I'm about to go into business with? If there's the slightest hesitation or uncertainty, I move on to the next project, the next outcome.

But no matter what I'm working on, I always act with the end in mind first.

What result do *you* want? Is your answer, "I want $10,000, $100,000, $10 million"? It's good to dream big, but you also have to be realistic. If you're making $45,000 a year now, your chances of making $65,000 in a year are really good. So are your chances of making $75,000. Making $90,000 or even $100,000 is still in the realm of possibility.

Is the result possible? Can you go from $45,000 to $10 million in a year, in two, in three? Making a large sum like that is still possible but a bit more of a stretch unless you give yourself a realistic timeline. Work up six-month, one-year, five-year, and ten-year plans. Look at the short- and long-term realities and act accordingly.

How badly do you *want* the result? If you don't want the outcome with every fiber of your being, you won't get it. So decide and then act.

Remember!
There's one more thing to talk about before you
race for that outcome: your frame of mind. You have
to relax. Lose the fear. Lose the stress. Replace it
with passion, desire, and faith, which
will grow with each action.

Pick an Activity

Look at the word *activity*—what are the first three letters? Act. So go act. Do something today. Do something tomorrow. Do something the day after. Simple actions over time will get you to your goal. Now is the time to remember all those old sayings, ones like "The longest journey begins with the first step." Take your first step. There's another line I like: "How do you eat an elephant? One bite at a time." Take your first bite.

That's where RUBs go wrong. RUBs focus on the goal. Rich Idiots focus on the activities that will get them to their goal.

Everyone's got goals. So why doesn't everyone reach them? Because it's not about the goal—it's about the activity to get to that goal. Got it?

Do what I do: Every night before I go to bed I make a list of two or three activities I'm going to do the next day—activities that will bring me that much closer to my goal.

For example, suppose you want to buy your second piece of real estate. That's your goal. What are you going to do tomorrow to make it happen? What activities are you going to undertake? You could buy the newspaper and call about three or four likely properties. You could visit a bank and fill out the necessary paperwork to get prequalified for a mortgage. You could make an appointment to interview a real-estate attorney specializing in rental properties. Or you could act on all three.

Get a Grip

Take control of your money life right now. Write down all the money you have coming in and all the money going out. No matter how dark the picture, it's so much better to know than not to know. Rich Idiots aren't afraid of bad news; they're afraid of no news.

Next, take action to fix whatever's broken about your finances.

Finally, get organized. Get a file box and organize your important financial papers: your will, your insurance policies, your titles, any power of attorney, your trust documents. If you don't have something, contact your attorney or Pre-Paid Legal (you'll find this organization on my Web site, www.GetRichWithRobert.com) to get it done. Put your financial house in order, even if it's a really small one-room house. Act as if you had millions to manage—and you eventually will.

Reward and Adjust

The minute you achieve a goal or complete an action, reward yourself. That's huge. Not everyone gets to this stage. If you're not getting the results you hope for, don't give up. Adjust the goal and adjust the activity. Rich Idiots don't get to be Rich Idiots by following a straight path . . . they zig and zag before they get to true riches.

Cut Yourself Some Slack

Don't be so hard on yourself. Remember, you're learning. Getting rich is a process. For example, when I make an offer on a property and get rejected, I'm not upset. Rather, I'm happy because I realize I didn't offer too much!

All information is feedback. All feedback is good. I've started businesses that failed, but afterward I sat back and said, "Great, let's see what you've learned and what you can apply to your next business." I've had real-estate investments and stock investments that didn't pan out the way I'd hoped, but I sat back and said, "Good job, Robert, let's see what you learned that you can apply to your next investment."

When I first started out I had to make a lot of cold calls. I hated cold-calling. But I knew that for every hundred calls I made, ten people I connected with would buy from me, and those ten meant sales, income, and bonuses. What did I do when thirty or forty people slammed the phone down? I said, "Hey, Robert, you're forty calls closer to your ten sales." That's the Rich Idiot mentality.

Keep on Keeping On

Enjoy the journey. Don't get discouraged. Most RUBs try something once and when it doesn't work out, they curl up in a little failure ball and never try again. But the fun is in the trying. The fun is in the game. Talk to any Rich Idiot and they'll tell you. The best part of the wealth, the billion-dollar business, the multimillion-dollar stock portfolio, the apartment complexes and shopping malls was the challenge of making it happen. It was the getting there.

You've stayed with the book this long, so you're in the game already. Just keep going after you've turned the last page. Because that's when your *real* fun will begin. Let me tell you, that's going to be the best ride of your life—your ride to riches.

Remember!
As I've been told by some of the world's great spiritual leaders, whom I've had the privilege to meet, people are far too hard on themselves. So feel good. Enjoy it all.

The Surprise Ending

I have one last secret for you. It's in the answer to a question I'm about to ask you. Get it right and you're on your way to becoming the next Rich Idiot. Get it wrong and you stay a RUB. Ready? Here's the question.

There are two people reading this book. One is going to remain a RUB and one is going to be the next Rich Idiot. What's the one thing that will make the difference? Turn the page for the answer.

The one who's still reading is the RUB.

The one who's already taken action or is going to take action is the next Rich Idiot.

Which one are you?

Thirty Rich Idiot Actions

Here are thirty immediate actions to follow, gathered from every single chapter of this book. Perform one a day and in just thirty days you'll be closer to your Rich Idiot dream!

1. Design your perfect life—that's your map.
2. Build your first Dream Team.
3. Forgive others. Forgive yourself.
4. Practice getting and receiving.
5. Practice giving generously.
6. Express gratitude for all that you have and all that you will have.
7. Believe in the abundance of the Universe.
8. Write down your one goal.
9. Write yourself a wealth check.
10. Write your mission statement.
11. Live rich today.
12. Make a wealth wall.
13. Look for "found" money.
14. Lose the toxic people in your life.
15. Take an inventory of your assets.
16. Take an inventory of your liabilities.
17. Make a list of your bad debt.
18. Make a plan to pay off your bad debt.
19. Make a list of your good debt.
20. Make a plan to acquire more good debt.
21. If you rent, buy your first house. If you own a house, buy your next one.

22. Buy a mutual fund.

23. Write your simple business plan.

24. Write down what you love to do—then do it.

25. Decide on the outcome you want.

26. Write down three activities you'll do every day to reach your goal.

27. Commit to a realistic time frame.

28. Write a schedule for yourself and keep to it.

29. Make a blessings list and say thank you for each one.

30. Have fun.

What do you do next? Visit my Web site, www.GetRichWithRobert. com, and find out!

bonus secret no. 8

You're Rich Already!

If only the people who worry about their liabilities would think about the riches they do possess, they would stop worrying. Would you sell both your eyes for a million dollars, or your legs, or your hands, or your hearing? Add up what you do have, and you'll find that you won't sell them for all the gold in the world. The best things in life are yours, if you can appreciate yourself.
— DALE CARNEGIE

You've Already Got Riches

Now, let me explain this. You may not feel rich right this minute, because you have responsibilities and rent or mortgage and car payments and all that stuff, but look at the big picture. You know, in the space of gratitude nothing else can exist.

Be Grateful for What You Have

If you're grateful for what you have, you'll feel wealthy and the Universe will smile on you. The reality is, you really are rich already.

Think about this. A lot of you may not have had the opportunity I've had to travel all over the world. You may not have seen how a lot of people live. The terrible reality is that the world is filled with people who don't have anything. The number of families trying to survive on pennies a day is incomprehensible. They don't have food. They don't have medicine. They don't have air-conditioning. They don't have cell phones. They don't have cars, credit cards, or books about how to become a Rich Idiot.

You may be struggling, too. You may be worried about your own family. You may be tossing and turning, thinking the kids are growing out of sneakers faster than you can buy them, that you're living paycheck to paycheck, that your rent is late and it's costing you a small fortune to fill your gas tank. You may think you can't do anything about it. But you *can* do something. You can be grateful for what you have already. And in expressing that gratitude you can open yourself to receiving even more gifts.

Do an inventory of what you *do* have: food, shelter, clothing, medicine. You've probably got enough food for dinner—and breakfast. You've probably got enough money for Starbucks on the way to work. You've got a job and a paycheck. You've got a roof over your head. You've got a cell phone, a computer, a TV, maybe an iPod, perhaps a DVD player or VCR. You've got more than one outfit in the closet, and all you ladies, I know you've got more than one pair of shoes, right? What else? You've probably got a washer and dryer to clean your dirty clothes, a dishwasher to clean your dirty dishes, a fridge to keep your food fresh, and a stove or microwave to heat it. There are sheets on your bed and a rug under your feet. The toilet flushes and the shower works. Your garbage gets picked up and your sewage is sanitized. Your water is safe and . . . you get the picture. You have a lot to be grateful for, as we all do.

You know, one of the reasons I travel to the Third World and do charity work is that it puts my life in perspective. When I see the pain and suffering of others I know I have no problems—just gifts.

My suggestion is that you take five minutes every day and count your blessings—then say "thank you" for having blessings to count.

And you know what will happen? Your own fears will disappear. You won't be stressed out or depressed. You won't be in a bad mood.

Your worries and anxieties will drop away. You'll feel lighter. You'll be open to all the goodies the Universe has just waiting for you.

True wealth doesn't come from having money, or stocks and bonds, or real estate. True wealth comes from gratitude for the things that really count.

To be a real Rich Idiot, you've got to know and appreciate what's truly important. It's that knowing that made me the Rich Idiot you're reading about now.

What got me started on the path to becoming a Rich Idiot was my boss's refusal to let me take off the day after Thanksgiving to count my blessings and be with my family. My boss asked, "Robert, where are your priorities? Obviously your priorities are not with your career or this company." And I replied, "You're right. My priorities are not with my career. They're with my family." In that instant I became a Rich Idiot and never looked back.

Those are your real riches. Your family, your friends, your health, your freedom, and your appreciation for what you have already and the gifts that are yet to come.

Each day comes bearing its own gifts. Untie the ribbons.
— RUTH ANN SCHABACKER

Extras to Help You As You Travel the "Rich Idiot" Path

One way to learn more about the principles discussed in this book is to click on my Web site:

www.GetRichWithRobert.com

Or call:

888-302-8018

You'll also find information there about how to attend seminars I regularly give—events that enable me to tackle all of the topics I cover here, but in a more interactive way that may prove useful. Certainly, I've received a great response as I've toured the country the past few years teaching Rich Idiot principles.

I happen to agree with scientists who believe each of us has a unique learning style. For some of us, book learning is *the* way to get necessary information. For such folks, books are priceless. After a tough start in life learning to read properly, I came to view books that way. But some people require additional learning tools, and that's why I'll always be committed to getting out there on the road and meeting people face-to-face.

For those who enjoy both my books and my seminars, but value the energy that comes from being part of a community built around the Rich Idiot philosophy, I've created an online multiplayer "Rich Idiot" game that will speed your progress and, best of all, is loads of fun. I've even built in some terrific extra incentives for winning that will breed spirited competition with your fellow contestants.

Check it out! It's all there on the Web site. And keep traveling the Rich Idiot path. One day you'll wake up and realize it's time to show someone *else* how to do it.